THE NARROW WAY HOME

A Collection of Thought Provoking Poems

Randolph Foltz

Copyright © 2013 by Randolph Foltz

The Narrow Way Home
A Collection of Thought Provoking Poems
by Randolph Foltz

Printed in the United States of America

ISBN 9781628395563

All rights reserved solely by the author. The author guarantees all contents are original and do not infringe upon the legal rights of any other person or work. No part of this book may be reproduced in any form without the permission of the author. The views expressed in this book are not necessarily those of the publisher.

Unless otherwise indicated, Bible quotations are taken from the King James Version (KJV) – *public domain*

www.xulonpress.com

To
Bob & Cathie
We need an outlet for
"OUR OLE AGE"
While Piding for you
poetry was me.

Randy Huff

Dedicated to:

Pastor James D. Bailey

He taught the Bible fundamentally.

In Memory of his most gracious and influential wife,

Judith C. Bailey

Also to:

Ms. Dorothy Rothgeb,

She generously gave of her time to teach a home Bible study

for 4 ½ years. She remains a true friend.

May God richly bless these folks

who have started us off in the right direction.

Acknowledgement

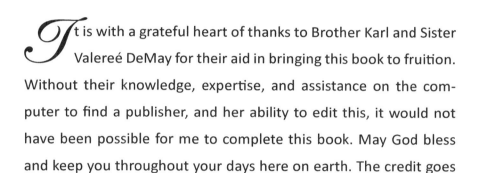

It is with a grateful heart of thanks to Brother Karl and Sister Valereé DeMay for their aid in bringing this book to fruition. Without their knowledge, expertise, and assistance on the computer to find a publisher, and her ability to edit this, it would not have been possible for me to complete this book. May God bless and keep you throughout your days here on earth. The credit goes to you two through our Lord and Savior.

Valereé, with my inability in English grammar, maybe you could drive it home with a hammer, and Karl, your help on the computer is one big job. I just don't understand, and often, I need a jog.

It is hard to teach an "ole dog new tricks". When one gets to be my age, learning doesn't often stick. I depend on the Lord and others, our good Christian sisters and brothers.

From Immaturity to Maturity

---

*B*eing born as immature babies, we develop to the mature adult in stages that take many years. We have the sin nature that came upon us beginning in the Garden of Eden. Satan deceived Eve into eating of the forbidden fruit, and Adam became involved for he was given Eve as a help meet and should have forbidden the act as the head of the family.

As babies, we have selfish natures. We continue to want our selfish needs met immediately, or we rebel by crying. Later on in life, we react in ways that try to attract the attention of those wants from any who will provide our needs.

I will not go into the many ways we adults make these challenges, but I will make an effort to elaborate on my position in this time of life. Some may be of the idea that strange and odd occurrences take place in old age. While I cannot disagree with this idea or thought, it does not necessarily happen to all. Some imbalances do take place in each of us in different ways.

As you read this tract, please be in the frame of mind that I am not or never have been more coherent. Though I may be somewhat forgetful at times, my thinking has never been better than now. I have not gone off the deep end, and I can still swim if necessary. My continuous reading, studying, hearing the preaching of the Bible, from studious preachers and teachers who are called by God to disperse His Word, also gives me confidence of this maturity.

When reading this, you may think this is not for you. The older I get the more I hear of this time and era we are living in, and the more I believe in the Bible. With the proper teaching and understanding you will have to agree that this nation and world is heading in the direction of destruction. There are entirely too many things that are occurring as prophesied in the Bible not to believe.

It is for these reasons I feel that I am mature and qualified enough to make suggestions and to help someone in need to see the way that leads to a "Life With Eternal Benefits".

The Journey of a Lost Man Traveling
The Broad Road

———⸺✑⸺———

I grew up as a young lad in a rural setting during the Great Depression. Many sought employment or did what they could to support their families. It was a difficult time for most Americans. My father was fortunate enough to start a country store and to work in the J.I. Triplett Flour Mill. My mother took care of the store during the day. Others were not as lucky, but most families had gardens and would can or store excess produce in their root cellars. Men would hunt, fish, or trap which often required early morning treks in all kinds of weather. The men would kill the catch and bring it home to be skinned, dried, and sold for a good market price.

On one night's hunt, I became lost. Although this even took place nearly 65 years ago, I vividly remember it. I spent a frightful night alone, without even a star to light my way. I felt very helpless, but this incident did not cause me to call out to the Lord. Eventually, someone found me and led me to safety.

As I grew older, I became rebellious. I joined the Army, thinking I could do as I pleased, yet this turned out to a mistake. In the military there was always someone telling me what to do. My assignment to the battlefields of Korea was not of my choosing. It was there that I was introduced to complete destruction.

Three buddies and I went out to retrieve a piece of equipment from the battlefront when we were pinned down by mortar fire. A round landed in a ravine just across from where we had taken cover, and a piece of shrapnel came straight toward us. It landed in the bank about six inches from my head. It could have killed me except God had other plans.

After leaving the service, my family and I vacationed in New York City. On the observation deck of the Empire State Building, I became conscious of how tiny all the people below seemed. At that point, I realized how insignificant I was to the world. This fact was a terrible blow to my ego. I turned to alcohol, an addiction that cost me more than I ever expected. Not only did the alcohol take a toll on my thinking, it also affected those who loved and tried to help me. The addiction caused me to eventually lose my house, property, finances, and even my family.

Being young and not knowing what life was all about brought many questions to mind: Why did I do the things I did? Where was God? Why did my father make me go to church as a child when he did not go himself? How did life fit in with what God had for me?

My second wife helped me see the foolish, short-lived pleasure of alcohol. The circumstances that God placed in my life caused me to see my helplessness and that Christ was the only answer. I had spent most of my life on the wrong road. Jesus said in Matthew 7:13-14, "Enter ye in at the strait gate; for wide is the gate, and broad is the way, that leadeth to destruction, and many there be which go in thereat; Because strait is the gate, and narrow is the way, which leadeth unto life, and few there be that find it." Praise God, He allowed me to make a U-turn.

God watched over me through childhood into my senior years. My family sent a teacher who introduced me to the Bible. My eyes were opened to the fact that the world was in darkness, and I was walking in darkness. In John 8:12, Jesus said: "I am the light of the world: he that followeth me shall not walk in darkness, but shall have the light of life." The Scriptures opened my eyes to my sin. I knew that I needed to change directions. I had to ask Jesus to forgive my sins, trust Him, and follow where He led me.

II Corinthians 5:17 states: "Therefore if any man be in Christ, he is a new creature; old things are passed away; behold, all things are become new." This is what took place in my life when I decided to accept Christ as my Lord and Savior. My new life caused me to see the wickedness of alcohol, smoking, and foul language. This new life called for a new set of friends. God truly changed me from the inside out and set me on a new road. God gave me peace and hope beyond comprehension and has blessed me beyond measure.

I was lost on the *broad road* that leads to destruction until I asked the Lord to forgive me and save me. My life is an example of the fact that God allows men to make U-turns. Every man starts out on the *broad road*, but God gives him signs so that he realizes where he is and allows him to make the U-turn that will get him on the *narrow road* that leads to life everlasting.

If you do not know the Lord, please take this opportunity to ask Jesus to forgive your sins and save you from an eternity in Hell. Jesus loves you so much that He left Heaven's glory, died on the cross, was buried, and rose from the dead to make the payment for your sins.

Psalm 14:1 and Psalm 53:1 say: "The fool hath said in his heart, there is no God". My life and testimony certainly prove that to be true. God said it (it's in the Bible), and I believe it.

The Broad and Narrow Way

Are you in turmoil, full of sadness and sin?
You don't know how this happened or just when
Happiness seems so very far away
You wonder, "How can I have a new day?"
On a broad road filled with potholes and challenges that lead to corruption
Heading straight to one that ends in destruction

Stop, Look, & Listen

Around the corner a new life glistens
There is a new way
Make a U-turn, get on the right road, the *narrow way*
It will lead you to a new life to face
One with relief, happiness, peace, and grace
You will soon learn
The rewards of the U-turn
Go with a smile and complete contentment
Let all know that it is God-sent

The Narrow Way Home

So much depends on how you spend your life

Do it with ease and not with strife

Making the turn onto the narrow way

Means with God you will forever stay

Section I

To the Christian or the Christian to be

Comes out of darkness to the Light of the World
If a man does not love his brother, he is a liar and the truth is not in him.

Learning God's Way

As a youngster, my education wasn't much
Many years later I found out Jesus was always in touch
In Sunday school I was introduced to Jesus,
but it didn't enter my heart
This is not the way for a Christian to start

Nearly a half century later while walking in the world of sin
Realizing that at any time my life could end
Telling my wife we needed to change our ways
We decided to see what the Bible had to say

Getting back into church we were not getting what we ought
Then we found a home teacher who knew
what we needed to be taught
After a year or two, we learned it was Jesus we wanted to please
But to do it right we would have to get down on our knees
And we did side by side before a preacher on TV

Confessing to Jesus the sinners that we were
He gave us His best
He removed those sins as far as the east is from the west
Commanding that in His Word we must stay
Reading and studying it each and every day

Some 30 years plus we still keep His Word before us
Because we know He is the one and the only one we can trust
And daily prayers are really a must
Keep us fresh and our minds from the form of rust.

It is quite plain to see an education is a good thing
But for salvation we need to depend on the King
So we attend church three times a week and join and sing
Giving peace and joy to our hearts and glory to God that it brings
By doing it God's way, it's there forever to stay.

rfoltz 9/20/2010

From the Heart and Mind of Man

When the mind gets the wonder lust
The heart says, "Look to Jesus, it's a must."
The mind desires to continue on
The heart will no longer belong

From the heart, "Jesus is the only way"
Yet the mind will fight to sway
Trying to get the heart to give in
In this mindset world of sin

Don't let the mind lead you down the wrong path
It could shorten your life in half
Let the heart have complete control
To determine the direction of your soul

rfoltz 3/2002

A True Friend

There is a friend

The truest of true

Who will be there until the end

Keep your chin up, don't be blue

The comfort He can give

He will offer to you

If His way you will live

He'll drive away the strife

This friend is Jesus who gave us life

rfoltz 9/2001

God, Family, and Country

God made it this way right in the beginning
The Bible tells God made everything — the Heaven and Earth
Right down to Revelation, the ending
Of Adam and Eve and all their worth

After the Creation, then came Adam
From a rib He made Eve
A fallen angel named Satan entered in
Causing Adam and Eve to be deceived
By eating of the fruit thus the beginning of sin

There they gave birth to Cain and Abel
The start of the family
They now had two more to set at the table
As a witness and would be more for the world to see

God's Word says He is a jealous God
He wants no other god to try and take His place
Or to lay claim to even a little piece of His sod
Or anyone in an area where He can trace

Father and mother who are to raise their child
As the Bible teaches
The Bible makes it all worth while
If into their heart it reaches

When they are old they will not depart from it
If when they are young they may stray
Have patience, they will return and not quit
And God will accept them never again to go away

rfoltz 9/20/2010

His Word in Your Heart

"Thy Word have I hid in mine heart,
That I might not sin against thee."
Always willing to help a lost soul get a start
To be relieved from their misery

There are none good, no, not one
We are just a ball of miry clay
Jesus, God's only Son
He can change that, Do it today

God sent Him to earth to become man
Who changed the sacrifice of blood
Giving us the Church, another clan
From those saved during the Great Flood

Jesus said, "I am the way, the truth, and the life
No man comes to the Father, but by me."
One no longer needs suffer strife
Believe on Him and some day face to face you will be

Reading the Bible and praying, doing your part

Sharing with the world His Word, the Gospel

All that is hidden in your heart

Depending on Jesus, that makes it possible

Proverbs 16:9

A man's heart deviseth his way: but the LORD directeth his steps.

rfoltz 3/2002

Standing Firm

Poetry from the heart and mind of man
Let us remember as our churches gather throughout this land
Be sincere and take a firm stand
For Jesus and this nation as best we can

We have suffered a severe blow
Returning to normal will be very slow
Don't be brought down so low
Be firm, let your Christianity show

rfoltz 10/01

From Darkness into Light

In darkness, blinded I couldn't see
Just what the evil influence had done to me
I stumbled and went to the lowest ebb
Floundering and struggling in a tangled web
What happened to a worldly one, I couldn't conceive
It was all because I didn't believe
Jesus came and took me in
Delivered me from this harried world of sin
Out of darkness into the light
Jesus gave to me spiritual sight
The world looks so different now
Humbly my head I bow
When all seems so dark, I now can see
Just what can be done for a sinner like me
Trust in the Lord and darkness will flee

rfoltz 4/02

Let your conversation be without covetousness; and be content with such things as ye have: for he hath said, I will never leave thee, nor forsake thee. Hebrews 13:5

A Gift

God gave me the gift
To write a book
To help others with a lift
If they will only look

It is a book of poems
It may help them see
How to drive it home
A Christian to be

A way of righteousness
To enter our hearts
Giving nothing more or nothing less
Sharing with others and a willing to depart

This most important choice
It's ours to make
That we can humbly voice
Let's not be left in a burning lake
Do it now, today's the date
Tomorrow could be too late

rfoltz 9/2001

Sharing With Others

Listen all you sinners and you shall hear
A great story of one who can remove all fear
Of one who had a very humble beginning
He can touch each and every one and will have no ending

Growing to have a short ministry with no sin in His life
But He can help all to remove their strife
He is one without any pride
Some day He will return for the church to be His bride

Calling twelve to share and spread His word
So around the world His story will be forever heard
Even though He was tried, no sin in Him could be found
He took the sin of the world that "whosoever will"
can be heaven bound

Yes, He was sentenced to death on a wooden cross
So everyone, you and I would not have to suffer loss
He's in heaven preparing for us a place
So the saved can meet Him face to face

You need to accept the Savior and with Him make your peace
Then as you go through the pearly gates be
prepared to a heavenly feast
The New Testament tells the whole story and
is expounded upon by Paul
How to each and every sinner He has given a call

Because of His mercy and grace
He is always ready to accept us without a chase
As we celebrate His birth on Christmas morn
Always read to share with others the reason baby Jesus was born

rfoltz 11/2002

What Would Christmas Be?

What would Christmas be
Without a Christmas tree?
Decorated all beautifully and in glory
Giving forth the Christmas story

The ornaments and many strings of lights
Filling the hearts of the admirers full of delights
Topped by a shining star
That guided the Wise Men from afar

Or maybe an angel looking down from above
Sending from God's Son His love
Reminding us of the coming year
Because of Him we are filled with cheer

The Christmas tree gives reason to tell
A story we love so well!

rfoltz 12/3/2004

Reason for An Attitude

Some say there are many "Reasons for the Season"
But there really is only one
That's Jesus, God's only son

He made possible everything
Let's rejoice and sing
If we are safe, sound, and secure without fear
It's because Jesus is very near

He furnishes us all our needs and wants
While encouraging us not to do the "Don'ts"
Go to Him on bended knees
Offering up our prayers, please

Always giving thanks for so very much
Directing us always to keep in touch
May every day be Thanksgiving Day
As we gather together to pray
Now and forever with an attitude
filled with gratitude

rfoltz 11/24/04

A Youth Report

At our church we appreciate our youth
Who gather often to learn the truth
They are able to shed the fears
That come to them from their peers
Enabling them to become leaders of tomorrow
Gleaning all the expertise from Scriptures they can borrow
As leaders learning to share
Teaching others how their burdens to bear
We sure do appreciate Pastor Chad and Becky for the job they do
Here at Valley Baptist Church, Radio and Christian School
All the activities they plan
Helps so much to keep them in hand
The Lord has in store for them many jewels for their crowns
For picking up those that had been left down
We pray they will keep up the good report
The church is behind them with one hundred percent support

rfoltz 10/2001

The Christian Awards

When a Christian gets out of God's will
In us His way He will instill
Knowing He is always there
Take these needs to Him in prayer

Do we now and then get out of line?
May the Holy Spirit convict us one more time
Reinstall in us a much-needed faith
Which for a Christian should be a natural trait

Humbly go to God and plead
To help you overcome this need
But don't put God to the test
He will always give you His best

The Lord's watching to see what we do
He is keeping an eye on me and you
There is coming an awarding day
We Christians must be careful what we do and say

rfoltz 11/12

Boldness From the Lord

Praying, I ask the Lord to help me out
With boldness I'm having a bout
Not being aware Jesus gave me the clout
His Word I can no longer doubt

He provides everything I will need
Including how to accomplish this deed
If on God's Word I'd continually feed
In witnessing to others, how to plead

Furnished a word processor I didn't know how to use
Inspired to write a book was the way to choose
Coming to the Lord so their souls not lose
And boldness to speak out was the only dues

rfoltz 11/16/2001

Isaiah 40:8 Green Grows the Grass

Green grows the grass and the flowers
As they beautify this world of ours
Just like life they fade away
But God's Word is here to stay

God inspired it, He breathed into man
Right from the beginning it was His plan
It was given so we could understand
That all could be saved throughout the land

Yes, we must read it, hide it in our heart
Be firm in it right from the start
So at any time we will be able to depart
His Word, it will keep us from Satan's hearth

The beauty of the flowers as they bloom
In heaven there is plenty of room
Make your reservation, make it soon
From the Sunday school hour, do it before noon

We won't fade away as the grass and flowers do
That is God's promise, don't be a fool
Into heaven He will accept me and you
But on earth He will use us as a tool

Isaiah 40:8
The grass withereth, the flower fadeth:
but the word of our God shall stand for ever.

rfoltz 6/2001

Do You Have a Full Deck?

I examined myself, I didn't have a full deck
I'll change, don't want that around my neck
Jesus, He did agree
He quickly accepted my plea

Soon a new person I found
Cause Jesus had turned me around
How much happier I am and my wife
Since I entered into this new life

I hope your deck is full
With Jesus, it doesn't take much pull
He'll accept you and take you in
And help to keep from the world of sin

rfoltz 6/2001

Judgment Day is Coming

Having each day a devotion
I often get the notion
Just where are we in Bible prophecy?
How near when we will enter into eternity?

In 1948 Israel became a nation, the Jewish home
They are returning from where they did roam
The Bible has much to say about the end times
To know these things, Luke 21 gives us many signs

Fewer and fewer are attending preaching
Getting further and further from Bible teaching
The world is really becoming a very sinful place
Even though we know soon a judgment we must face

Our prayers for each and every one
Is to accept Jesus Christ the Son
As we should have already learned
We are anxious for Jesus to soon return

rfoltz 6/2001

The Guiding Hand

Moses was instructed to take a trip
He would at all time be properly equipped
This was to the Promised Land
A part of God's plan
Knowing not it would take 40 years
Or that the land was very near
They traveled by a pillar of cloud by day
And a pillar of fire at night to show the way
Though fed with manna and quail they complained
They wanted not to suffer pain
This must have been quite a shock
Lead on and camping by the sea
As Pharaoh pursued, turning back was their plea
Directed to lead on he was told by God
Stretch out your hand and lift your rod
The waters parted and formed a wall they found
And they crossed over on dry ground
Pharaoh pursuing, closely he followed
When the waters came together, his army was swallowed
Now as we are directed and by God are told

Whatever it is we need to be bold

We are to follow his directions

If we want His corrections

He's always available to show us the way

And we are invited to be with Him and permanently stay

Psalm 32:8

I will instruct thee and teach thee in the way which thou shalt go: I will guide thee with mine eye.

rfoltz 7/2001

A Great Love

God's great love for us
We're never satisfied we fuss
When we are down
You take away the frown
Causing us to look up
Remembering the promise of the communion cup
You showed us how undeserving we are
By turning a thorn into a flower
There are many earthly pleasures
But in heaven we place our treasures
Though we may fuss and frown
Your love for us will never let us down

rfoltz 7/2001

Don't Fear

The lightning flashed, the winds blew in a violent rainstorm
Don't fear, Jesus will carry you in His arms
Threats from a wicked world of bodily harm
Don't fear, Jesus will carry you in His arms
The world falls around you taking away your charm
Don't fear, Jesus will carry you in His arms
No matter the challenge, there is no reason for alarm
Just call on Jesus, He'll take you in His arms
Things happen bringing on stress
Look to Jesus, He'll give you His rest
When burdens on your shoulders do fall
Get on your knees and give Jesus a call
Whenever you think there is fear
Remember Jesus, He is always very near
He's patiently awaits to hear your prayer
We can depend on Him, He's always there
Now when all these problems to me came
Jesus answered my prayers and for you He'll do the same

rfoltz 7/2001

The Bill's Paid

Jesus was tried, convicted and hung on a cross
Not knowing He was "The King of Kings", the Boss
It was the world's gain
By Him having to suffer pain
Through a most despicable action
A substitute for sin brought satisfaction
And gave an easier way to salvation
Establishing an eternal relation
Yes, Jesus was hung on a cross
For all who accepted Him, He paid the cost
He paid in full the bill
By doing His Father's will

rfoltz 8/2001

Let's Be Bold

Let's be bold

To help save a soul

Do it without a doubt

Bravely speak out

Do it without fear

The Lord is always near

You may keep one from falling

To hear the Lord calling

"Come be with Me

For all eternity"

To me someone was bold

That helped save my soul

rfoltz 9/2001

Good Morning!
It's Sunday School Time
Let's Open with a Little Rhyme

It's 9:30 Sunday morn
Aren't you glad you were born?
Another great day the Lord has made
As into God's Word we wade
Set your mind, become engaged
Open your Bible to the right page
We pray there is a yearning
Of God's Word, more to be learning
Hope you have your Bible, God's tool
A most important need for Sunday School

As we depart from here today
Will we be able to say
We are better equipped to witness?
Because we really listened
Will we add another jewel to our crown
And not let God down
Let's be serious, be no fool
And learn from Sunday school

rfoltz 8/2001

Dialing Heaven

Someone is always on the line
With God that's okay, call anytime
You can be on your face or on your knees
At such trying times as these
Just don't give up, please
Give to God your request
He'll answer in His time, He knows best
Cause sometimes it may be only a test
When there is a need, don't hesitate
You can never be too late
God's nature is not to hate
You'll find happiness and joy
For men, women and girls and boys
What we may think is too big for God, to Him it's only a toy
Dial anytime, you'll get a pure answer without the leaven
This is a direct line to heaven

rfoltz 8/2001

God Our Provider

God will give us our needs
Not always our pleads
Sometimes our wants
But never His don'ts
If the valley is deep and dark,
He'll make a spark
There will always be hope
His promises we can quote
It could be much labor
Help will come from a neighbor
So open your heart and sing
Let the joy bells ring
Send your prayers to God above
They will be answered because of His love

rfoltz 9/2001

**God will never let you down
Without a way to pick you up**

You're in Our Prayers

Heard you were under the weather
We are praying you will soon be better
You are missed sitting in your pew
Not by a couple, but quite a few
We know you are in God's hand
Helping to fulfill His plan
We keep you in our prayers
Knowing for you God really cares
For one who has been so faithful and true
He will always be looking out for you

rfoltz 9/2001

VBVBS

North, East, West, and South the buses are outbound
Wherever there are children to be found
To join in this pool
Of children at Valley Baptist Vacation Bible School

For five days each evening they make this trip
They will find teachers who are ready and equipped
All them serious, no time to fool
At Valley Baptist Vacation Bible School

Games and entertainment for each girl and lad
And for all there are refreshments to be had
Those driving by have reason to drool
Because they are not in Valley Baptist Vacation Bible School

Accepting Jesus is their theme
Teaching them the right way is no dream
The ways of sin is the way of a fool
We don't want that at Valley Baptist Vacation Bible School

They will learn of Jesus and how to pray
That will lead them to heaven someday
With friends and neighbors in heaven they
won't have to lose their cool
They were blessed at Valley Baptist Vacation Bible School

Proverbs 22:6

Train up a child in the way he should go: and when he is old, he will not depart from it.

rfoltz 7/2001

A Theme with a Cure

The theme of the Bible is salvation
Christians are to take it around the world
To each and every nation
Wherever we are, let the Christian flag unfurl

We are to wear the full armor of God
Prepared to fight evil from all High Places
Wearing the proper equipment, our feet well shod
Fighting the evil of all willing to face us

The loins all girded with truth
And the breastplate of righteousness
The sword of the Spirit "God's Word" as proof
To ward off the evil of those who try to caress us

God's Word tells how we are to walk
Knowledge of the Scriptures shows how to act
Always being prepared with whom we talk
If from the Bible we can quote it as a fact

Jesus is the true Light
He will light our path
And keep us from the darkness of night
Away from Satan we can turn and laugh

As long as Jesus is at our side
He'll protect us from an evil attack
While walking upright if in Him we'll abide
He'll give us the strength, for any we lack

Always we should yearn
To keep a heart that's true and pure
Looking at His Word, more to learn
We can find the answer and cure

rfoltz 7/2001

Are You Adopted?

Are you an adopted one
Through Jesus Christ the Son?
We are told how in the book of John
A part of this family we can become

Any advice I will give
Would be for Jesus, in us to live
Nothing could be more positive
He took our sins, is what He did

So if you think worldliness is pleasure
Try the Christian way as a measure
If adopted, that is something to treasure

rfoltz 8/2001

Heaven's My Home

I've entered heaven through the pearly gate
Please don't shed a tear
I avoided a fire in a lake
And it was Jesus who brought me here

As a disobedient sinner
Walking in those worldly ways
Thought I'd never enter
For my sinful days

Jesus makes a difference
If we only follow Him
He'll run for us interference
And will make us a gem

Being here in a perfect place
Leaving all the aches and pains behind
All the sinful ways no longer we have to face
Hope all my earthly friends get in line

To join in a truly great fellowship
And praise and worship the Lord forever
As quickly as a wink we make the trip
It happened so easy, hardly an endeavor

So if you don't know how
Check out the Romans Road
Then to Jesus your head do bow
Turn over to Him your full load

The verses are these:
Romans 3;23, 6:23, 5:8, 10:9
Now Jesus you will please
Believe on Him you'll be fine

John 3:16 will tell you why
Read your Bible each day
Because it does not lie
Then come to heaven to be with me to stay

rfoltz 8/2001

Boldness, It's a Command

You must be bold

The Bible says, when He saves your soul

It's part of the deal

Reaching others with His appeal

To come to Him

Do it without a whim

Go sound the alarm

To help divert many from eternal harm

Don't hide His Word in your pocket

Write in big, bold letters on the docket

Speak to everyone you can

For the Lord, take a firm stand

Spread salvation far and wide

We need to accept Him to be a part of the Bride

Some day we can abide

On the streets of gold

A promise from the Bible we're told

We only have one life to give

Turn it over to Him and forever live

Please don't delay

Go to Him, repent, and pray
Now is the time, do it today
Again, I say we must be bold
The Lord is interested in every soul

Romans 10:11
For the scripture saith, Whosoever believeth on him shall not be ashamed.

rfoltz 10/2001

Our Sunday School Class

In the last little while we've been learning many facts
All about Dr. Luke's book of Acts
Including Paul's conversion by a blinding light
Turning him around and getting things right
Tells of the church and its beginning
One that will have no ending
Also Paul's missionary journeys
Speaking God's Word was his yearning
Now we will go to the Book of John
Informing us that God and Jesus are one
Relates the need to be born again
To reach Heaven where there is no pain
The many miracles He did perform
Should in us set off an alarm
Pray for "Bob" as he gives us each lesson
Make it a priority to attend every session

rfoltz 10/2001

Cupid's Arrow

When hearts are pierced with Cupid's Arrow,

It gives directions that are straight and narrow

A way to spend a life

Whatever it may be, even choosing a wife

There is only one way to live

With a heart always ready to give

One that is filled with bountiful love

Which can only come from the Master, God above

rfoltz 1/02

The Answer

Thinking I was the worst sinner of all
Until I read in Acts about the Apostle Paul
About when he answered the call
Letting his sins on Jesus fall

My sins I asked for forgiveness of all of them
He accepted without a whim
They were causing my head to swim
And my life so very dim

Jesus made the difference in my life
Especially between me and my wife
Eliminating most of my strife
Nothing can separate us now, not even with a knife

In the Bible I found
The way to turn my life around
My old life is now out of bounds
While the world thinks I'm a clown

In John I learned of being born again
How it will rid me of most of the pain
Ephesians instructs us to put on the full "armor of God"
Then the old ways I will no longer trod

Casting aside the "ole me"
A new individual you will see
Following Jesus has set me free
Now I'm as happy as can be

Reading the Bible each and every day
Also going to the Lord to pray
Helps keep me in the right way
Because once there, it's forever to stay

When I went to Jesus and was sincere
He was no longer far off but very near
No longer do I have to fear
When I call on the Lord, He is always right here

You won't have to wait
He is always there and never late
Yes, He's always on time
And the answer may be in this rhyme

Precious Hope

Something more precious than diamonds, rubies, silver or gold
It is a family that knows the Lord has saved their souls
With this comfort, the mind can be set to rest
Knowing the Lord always knows what is best
Hope of heaven, a hope we can treasure
While on earth it will give much pleasure

rfoltz 1/14/02

Congratulations to a Deacon

Congratulations! You have met all the qualifications
To the Lord you have such a dedication

The deacon—an office many are seeking
One of honor and sincerity
To be served for all eternity
An extension of the Pastor's arm
With personality, ability, and a friendly charm
Provide the help to one in need
Just a part of the Deacon's deed
Always willing to worship and give praise
For a Christian family one is allowed to raise
To be in continued service to the Lord—what a delight!
And to help Christians with an on-going worldly fight
A dedicated heart will keep one in line
Willing and able to give the very best to the Lord anytime

rfoltz 1/02

Fulfilling a Need

We've gathered to fulfill a need
To help a sister is the deed
So as they sing these hymns
While helping her we are praising Him

Jesus that is, on whom we rely
May we fall on our knees and cry
Would you please send us the answer
Just how to cure this cancer

Yes, Lord we really do care
Let us be in constant prayer
We know you are always there
Our burdens to share

It's not like the telephone
We never get a busy tone
Meaning we are never alone
Jesus, we should be His clone

As they sing these songs planting a seed
From the young and the old they plead
For a love one who has a need
And Jesus will remember your deed

II Corinthians 9:8
And God is able to make all grace abound toward you;
that ye, always having all sufficiency in all things,
may abound to every good work:

rfoltz 10/01

He Took Me In

Walking in the deepest and vilest sin
I cried, "Help!"
Jesus forgave me and took me in
Then came fears accompanied with doubt
With His mercy, He pulled me out
Makes no difference how deep the clay
By His grace He'll pick you up to stay
There is no sin He won't forgive because of His love
God sent it to His Son in the form of a dove
How did it happen, where or when
Because of His mercy, grace, and love
He'll forgive your sin
He'll pick you up, dust you off, and take you in

rfoltz 10/01

The World is Not My Home

As the old song goes
"This world is not my home, I'm just passing through"
Jim's earthly journey is over – in heaven he will start anew
All the sorrow and pain left to those behind
Will slowly heal with time
So as you grieve and seek relief
Remember he is in heaven because of his belief
Jesus will remove all the ills and pain
Over in glory life is perfect and his suffering was not in vain
Just because life on earth for him is through
Make your peace with the Lord and someday
you can be with him, too

rfoltz 5/04

I'm No Longer a Slave

Before being saved
And not knowing how to behave
And living a life like an empty cave

Seems as it was driven
How can one be forgiven
For a sinful life they've been living

Dark, dreary, a miserable life
Overtaken by sinful strife
Could this be removed with one swipe

Being filled with sin
And not knowing where to begin
It was then that Jesus entered in

Jesus had been to the cross
He paid the entire cost
For all sinners, not only the lost

Go to the Lord and pray
Ask for forgiveness, do it today
Do not delay

"Lord, forgive me for all those sinful things
Fill my heart with the joy that it brings
Now and forever a new song we can sing"

I'm saved! Saved! Saved!
Now I know how to behave
To sin I'm no longer a slave

rfoltz 2/04

Cheers From Above

The Lord has called me home
To tread the streets of gold
No longer in the sinful world will I have to roam
Heaven is so beautiful almost more than I can behold

To those who are left behind
Please be cheerful and don't cry
The Lord has been so good and kind
He brought me here, don't wonder why

Be of comfort and rejoice
To know where I have gone
Smile and say, "I made the right choice"
And will be there with you before long

Always walk with God and be faithful and true
Go to the Lord each and every day
Asking Him to take care of you
For blessings as you pray

rfoltz 4/04

Good Morning; Thank you Lord

Good morning

Thank you for the night of rest

Thank you for the very best

Thank you as we start this day

Thank you for your Word to show us the way

Thank you to us you have been so good

Thank you for this food

Thank you for the health you have blessed us with

Thank you especially for salvation as a gift

Thank you for Jesus who forgives sins of all

Thank you that we can any time call

Thank you that our sins can quickly be forgiven

For the life we have been living

rfoltz 4/04

Are You Doing Your All?

We've had Sunday school

We've had preaching

Are we following its teaching?

Remember pass through these doors

As a born-again Christian

We owe the world much more

You walk the walk and talk the talk

Your witness should be one of righteousness

Always more and nothing less

Give it your very best

To pass the test

rfoltz 5/2002

My Plea for Forgiveness

Down through the years
I caused many tears
For the crudeness
For the rudeness
For the misery I brought
To those without thought
Or concern of my selfishness
So may I confess
Just how wrong I've been
To have committed such a sin
The Lord has forgiven me
Would you please forgive me?
It is my plea
I no longer remember the days of old
For the Lord has saved my soul

rfoltz 9/01

Forgive Us for the Delay

Mrs. Collins, please forgive us when we forget
It sure wasn't intentional, you can bet
We are asking of you for this delay
'Cause we wanted to really wish you a very Happy Birthday
Knowing this is number ninety-four
With you God has kept an open door
Going to the Lord a we pray
Asking God to keep using you each day
The crowns that await you will be plenty
For your influence to save souls have been many
Hoping you had the happiest birthday
What could be better than to be with the Lord to stay

rfoltz 6/03

A Reason for the Season

A joyful time of the season
God Himself gave us a special reason
What a gift He gave, a special one
His only child, His Son

Throughout the season and coming year
Let's all serve Him from the heart and without fear
As you missionaries serve not questioning "why"
You merely said, "Send me, here am I"

We are here with prayers in your support
Always glad to hear when you report
We're always ready to rejoice
When you tell us of one who made the Lord their choice

May the fruits of your labor reap many reward
From those who come to know the Lord
Stars galore will be in your crown
So many hardly enough room can be found

Bless you in the Lord's call

To serve Him wherever and without a flaw

We thank you for serving without a fuss

And going out representing all of us

Matthew 1:21

And she shall bring forth a son, and thou shalt call his name JESUS: for he shall save his people from their sins.

rfoltz 12/01

Peter, The Apostle

Peter, an apostle, one of the chosen few
Serving the Lord as Christians should do
Though he denied Him thrice, it was then the cock crew

He stood firm for the Savior though
His dedication as a witness he did show
Petra or Peter a solid rock his name gives reason to grow

As the captors for Jesus came near
He stood against them brave and without fear
Drawing his sword he cut off one's ear

After denying the Savior, he hung his head in shame
For he knew the reason Jesus came
It was to convert sinners, give them new life and a new name

With Jesus he did walk side by side
He was there with Him when He died
With many of the others he also cried

The New Testament gives two small chapters to him
He'd jump to conclusions quickly and without a whim
Sometimes by unbelievers he would be condemned.

He never stopped as he traveled from town to town
Teaching others their lives could be turned around
So at the pearly gates we will not be turned down

II Peter 1:1
Simon Peter, a servant and an apostle of Jesus Christ, to them that have obtained like precious faith with us through the righteousness of God and our Saviour Jesus Christ:

rfoltz 1/04

Thumbprints of Time

My grandfather, a man I greatly admired
Stood erect, gentle, and of kindness never tired
The impression he made on me
I wondered how, why could this be?
Opening his Bible that was handed to me
How plain it is, I can now see

Leafing through the well-used pages
Reading the Bible was his spiritual wages
There are words and verses underlined
He had read them over and over all the time
The Bible was his direction in life and to others he was always kind

On the upper left margin on each page there is a great stain
But I will never complain
Because that is the reason for this rhyme
That was proof of granddad's thumbprints of time

rfoltz 4/19/07

All the Day Long

When we feel down and want to pout
The Book, all the day long, get it out
Read a chapter or two
It helped me and will help you, too
If we live by faith, there's no doubt
A big "hallelujah" to the Lord we'll shout

rfoltz 12/00

He Leadeth Me

The Lord is my Shepherd
Come join the flock
Do it just now
We can't turn back the clock
He will lead you to pastures
With grass tender, pure, and green
Taking a guilt-stained heart
Washing it snow-white clean
With an outstretched staff
He'll gather you in
Removing a doubtful mind
From a world of sin
When the valley seems so deep and feeling very low
He will fill an empty cup causing it to overflow
Come join the Shepherd – be a part of the flock
Be on the ship where heaven will be its final dock

rfoltz 3/03

Jesus Watches and Cares

When we are mere babes in arms
Mom and Dad are nearby to answer all alarms
Whether it be a whimper or a loud cry
They come running to find out why

Growing older and time passes by
You may sometimes ask just why
Parents are there for you
Monitoring all the things you do

Then comes the day when you become of age
God will be looking at the actions you engage
He'll reach out to show one the way
To follow Him each and every day

He wants all to be just as His Son
Giving the direction as Jesus had done
Jesus never committed a sin
No matter the temptation, He never gave in

God is everywhere, we cannot escape
No matter where we go or the route that we take
Always remember, however we travel, or however we walk
Jesus sees all, even our talk

Sometimes we need to listen to ourselves
Don't just pluck any old thing off the shelf
Always keep in mind, always be aware
Jesus looks on at all times
He really does care

rfoltz 12/03

Comfort in an Ole Song
As the Sun Fades in the West

An ole song title, "This World is Not My Home, I'm Just Passing Through"
The earthly journey is over, in heaven one can start anew
As the sunlight of life fades behind the mountains in the west
God will now bestow upon one His very best
All sorrow and pain to those left behind
Will slowly heal with the passing of time
So as you grieve and seek relief
Remember, heaven is home because of belief
Jesus will now remove all the ills and pains
Over in glory land life is perfect and one will not have lived in vain
With passing of a love one life on earth is through
Someday you can join them and be there too
With the earthly journey over and life has faded away
Being with the Heavenly Father brings forth a brighter day

rfoltz 7/04

The Antagonizing 4 Letter Word

There is an antagonizing word that haunts most of us
Causing many to challenge in whom we put our trust
Sin raises its ugly head and makes a fuss
Then the Evil One tempts us to cuss
And that little antagonizing word is called lust

Satan has met one greater than he
The one who has set us free
He can override him to defeat
Turning that "little word" into a Christian treat
All a battle from that antagonizing word He won
Through Jesus, God's only begotten Son

rfoltz 2/22/10

A shadow from the heat
Isaiah 25:4

God Will Keep Us

God will take care of us
He'll do it without a fuss
But if we step out on our own
He may let us fall, even break a bone
Even then He won't leave us alone
As our bodies begin to mend
He'll continue to watch over us to the very end
When the valleys seem the deepest
The mountains seem the steepest
He finds a way to keep us
It's important if we want His care
To take everything to Him in prayer

rfoltz 1/02

A Prayer of Thanks and Hope

As I arise, getting out of bed
Looking to another day, by the Lord being led
Thank you for the night of rest
Being prepared for another day
I hope I pass the test
Reading the Bible each and every word
Gleaning from its pages every morsel and bit, whey, and curd
Ingesting it, its teaching the way of righteousness, its main attraction
With hope that there will be no infraction
Keeping our eyes stayed upon thee
That all will follow you, including me
Great will be the gratitude
For having a Godly attitude
Through faith there is instilled much hope
Otherwise life would always be a downward slope
Thanks for all the hope and promises
For removing us as doubting Thomases

rfoltz 5/30/02

Heaven is the Reward

You want to get to heaven
Let me tell how to do it
Have faith in Jesus, and He'll see to it
He'll take away all the guilt and sin
Prepare for you a place where life will never end
He'll pick you up and dust you off
While making you reservations in heaven's loft
He'll direct you and cause you to do
Things you never thought you could do
Trust in Him, and He'll see you through
He'll show you a new way to walk
Also give you a new way to talk
Heaven is just a prayer away
Where all the Saints will gather some day
God sent His Son to this sinful land
To remove the sins from man
So our trip to heaven is a part of His plan
Heaven is a most wonderful and awesome place
And there we will see Jesus face to face
Asking forgiveness is your ticket on the heaven-bound plane

Your life now will never be the same
Give Him glory and praise here on earth
Heaven will be the reward
What is it worth?

John 6:47
Verily, verily, I say unto you,
He that believeth on me hath everlasting life.

rfoltz 6/28/02

His Love Sent on the Wings of a Dove

Reading each day more and more
About a Savior and the sins He bore
Conquering man and his sinful fall
Offering freely salvation to one and all
To any who will accept Him
Receiving the Light that will never dim
The Light being Jesus Christ the Son
Through Him is the only way it is done
The rewards are many and come with a crown
Turning a sinful life upside down
For Him it was no chore
Faith in Him is always an open door
Because of the Holy Spirit and His redeeming love
Sent from heaven on the wings of a dove

rfoltz 7/11/02

The Evangelist's Call

Beckoning to the Evangelist, he came
Obediently, well prepared, he answered the call
With authority, iniquities he called by name
To everyone within hearing distance of the hall

The message was one of concern
To the unbelieving world, from God's Word he made it clear
It was to keep them from a place where they eternally burn
And the end times are very near

Always using the King James Bible
Preaching to all who would come
As it is God's Word and always reliable
No matter the walk of life you're from

Leaving, he left words to test the belief
As he travels throughout the USA
Helping all he comes in contact with from a life of unbelief
Witnessing to all who would listen along the way

The words you brought to us
Will strengthen our faith much more
And did it without a fuss
We are so much richer than before

Thanks to you and the family for being here
We will pray for you as you travel along the way
Remembering, to us you brought much cheer
And we hope you can return another day

rfoltz 9/02

From the Most Wanted to The Book of Life

Are you pictures among the most wanted?
My prayers are, you are not
But please do not be undaunted
There is a revealing plot

If you are pictured there
My prayers are you'll be apprehended
Jesus makes it very easy to bear
It is really highly recommended

The Advocate, Jesus, has taken the penalty for you
Life with Him will be the sentence
From the most wanted to the Book of Life
is what He will do
But only if you will come to Him in repentance

rfoltz 11/02

The Bible, God's Word

The Bible, God's Holy Word
So much many have not heard
From the days of old and to the new
It's for everyone not just a few
It teaches salvation for our souls
Entering your name on the Book of Life roll
A Christian life we are to live
And the offering we should give
God's promises, the Bible, is full of them
They are not there by a mere whim

Our needs will be met and fulfilled
Our sins to Jesus He did bill
There is no way we can outdo Him
Our works to the Lord are quite dim
The Bible tells Jesus is the one to follow
Then life will be much easier to swallow
Let's all devote our time to the Good Book
Let the Holy Spirit in us keep a close look
There is no question about it

Reading it we cannot doubt it
It is God's Holy Word
No one can say you haven't heard.

II Timothy 3:15-16
And that from a child thou hast known the holy scriptures,
which are able to make thee wise unto salvation
through faith which is in Christ Jesus.
All scripture is given by inspiration of God,
and is profitable for doctrine, for reproof, for correction,
for instruction in righteousness:

rfoltz 11/30

Lord, Take Us Home

Lord, come take us home
This wicked world we no longer want to roam
So very much wickedness
A Christian, this world cannot caress
We can no longer understand
Just what happened to this land
Your word in the Bible available to all
Yet so many won't heed and will fall
Many you've picked up from the miry clay
Turned them around and sent them another way
Let us pray while we are still here
Keep us from the world of fear
Witnessing to all in whom we come in contact
Faith in Thee they do lack
As the Savior of this land and across the foam
Lord, please hurry back and take us home

rfoltz 3/02

A Cheery Place

The church office is a cheery place
So much happens in such a small place
Always with a bright and smiling face
All because of God's grace

One needs to be on one's toes
Just to see how things go
For all the problems such as those
The answer is there in Miss Rose

There are so many different chores
Need solving and lots more
Most are serious and some folklore
Whatever the situation there is always an open door

There may be a concern to fill
Or maybe just to pay a bill
One ruling we must instill
It must be in God's will

rfoltz 3/02

From Sin to Another Goal

While walking down the path of sin
Jesus picked me up and took me in
But what now? Where do I begin?
Along came one who would teach me what to do

Keeping me from the way of a fool
Showing me the Bible, a most valuable tool
Realizing what a vile person such as I
Asking the Lord, "Why me Lord, why?"
Now I can raise my head and no longer cry

Learning there is a more precious way
With Jesus in my heart, that Satan cannot sway
Being in Jesus I'm there to stay

Going to church and being continually fed
Now knowing why Jesus bled
All those old sins are now dead

Speak up, be very bold
There should now be a most important goal
To reach out to others and help save a soul

Psalm 14:1
The fool hath said in his heart, There is no God. They are corrupt, they have done abominable works, there is none that doeth good.

rfoltz 3/02

The Gift of Light

Listen all my little children, sisters, brothers, and you shall hear
About a gift that is given this time of the year
Yes, it came down from heaven above
God's special gift of His Son because of His love
So as we ready for this gift-giving season
Remember in your heart that Jesus is really the reason
Of all the gifts that will be given
Jesus gave true meaning to the life we are living
He is the most precious gift and none can compare
For a Savior who is always there
To answer prayers we want done
He is the one when our hearts He has won
When we flounder and stagger in the darkest of night
The darkness will give way to Jesus, the one and only true light
In addition, to give us 2007 to face without fear
Let us make this the greatest and most cheerful day
By living all of life, the Jesus Way

rfoltz 11/21/2006

Wanta Get to Heaven? It's Just a Prayer Away

Wanta get to heaven? Let me tell you how to do it
Get out the Old King James Bible and get in to it
Find the book of John and chapter three
Where Jesus told Nicodemas, from sin how to be set free
Just by being "born again"
The Holy Spirit will take away the sin

So pray, pray, pray, each and every day
Keeping Satan at a distance is all I can say
Because heaven is just a prayer away

Go to Romans and take the Roman's Road
Romans 3:23 says, as a sinner we all carry a load
We come short of the glory of God
For all of us on this road have once trod
If we confess with our mouth that we believe
Jesus is quick of those sins to relieve

So pray, pray, pray, each and every day
To keep the devil, Satan, at bay
Cause heaven is just a prayer away

Jesus dies, was buried, and rose again from the grave
Romans 10:13 says that all who will call on Him will be saved
Oh, yes, hallelujah! We are born again
There is now a new person within
Where a long lost person once did live
God for us, His son did give

So pray, pray, pray, each and every day
Because we are now in Jesus' arms to stay
And heaven is just a prayer away

In Hebrews 10:25 we are told to assemble
Exhorting one another for Jesus to resemble
Reading His Word every day is a good way to start
Causing us to hide it in our heart
He will remove all the sin and pain
For we are now born again

Now heaven will be the final resting place
There we will be with Jesus forever face to face
Singing praises and giving glory to the great God above

For His mercy and grace He gave to the sinner with love

Rejoice, rejoice, rejoice! Again, I say
He will keep us from falling away
Cause heaven is just a prayer away

rfoltz 9/3/2009

Now that is about all there is to it
Get out the ole King James and get right to it
Do it now before it's too late
You will meet Jesus just inside the gate

rfoltz 8/8/2010

A Decision to Make

In each life there is a decision to make
If you want to get to heaven, which road to take
In the Bible Jesus gave His plan
This will keep us from Satan's hand
Get down on your knees
And Jesus will hear your pleas
Ask for forgiveness of all your sins
The heavenly gate will open and let you in

The time is now don't be too late
Because the Father only knows the date
When He will make that call
Don't linger, don't stumble, don't fall
Get aboard that heaven-bound train
And life will never be the same

Jesus has all the answers, He really cares
Through His great love, He wants all to be there
The road is not crowded, there is room for all
You will be secure, from His arms you will never fall

Making this choice will be a different walk
Anytime, anywhere, with Him you can talk
Yes, call on Him through your prayers
The line is never busy; He is always there
Your problems He hears for He is everywhere

Everything is possible with Jesus if we will call
He can answer our needs; nothing is too big or too small
What a loving Savior, He came to save you and me
Confused you ask, how can it be?
When God created the heavens and earth
He created man and woman to glorify His worth
Oh, there may some doubt how this could be done
The answer is simple just study the book of John

The time is now; don't be late
With Jesus make this date
Some day into eternity you fly away
Because of the decision you made today

rfoltz 9/9/2008

God's Created Man

God, from the dust of the earth created Adam – Man
Along with a book – The Bible – that will forever stand
From a rib of Adam He made Eve, a help meet, and wife
To propagate on earth more life
Giving him dominion over all the earth
Impressing on him of its worth.

In the Old Testament ten commandments are presented
For a Godly life to all who have repented
What, how and when, one should BELIEVE
God quickly, will forgive those sins into
His fold He will then RECEIVE.

He immediately gives Satan the sign
They are Christians! Their mine!
There will be many attempts to cause them to FALL
We must be constantly listening for God's call.

A new converted Christian has much obedience to learn
The ways of the world they must spurn
And we may be the only Bible they will ever read or hear
Becoming one of God's children will help remove their fear.
Show them how to get on their knees
And ask God to forgive them of all past sins, Please!
Be sincere, do it from the heart
Your life will now have a new start.

Yes, you will become a new person in God
As all before you, the sinful road they all have trod
You've been BLESSED by what JESUS has done
By God giving Him to cover your sins,
HIS ONLY SON!
This promise you can deposit in the Bank!
Giving them both a big THANKS!!

rfoltz 2/13/2013

Paul Answered the Call

On his way to Ole Damascus town
Annihilating all Christians he found
When suddenly he fell to his knees
Said to the Lord "what would you have me to do?" Please
It happen so quickly he lost sight
He didn't have time to put up a fight
It was here he saw the true light
The Lord said He would train him through and through
If going and preaching His word would he do
Oh how he traveled far and wide
Doing his best to win others to Christ, He continuously tried
Though ship-wrecked, stoned, and left to die,
imprisoned, he never quit
Remembering Jesus who had been tortured
and upon Him they did spit.
Though there was a thorn in the flesh
From his testimony one would never guess
His service to the Lord was his most important request

Though we may never get such a call
We can use him as an example "The Apostle Paul"!
Our words or testimony will never appear in God's Holy Word
Maybe in song like the "Wing of a Great Speckled Bird"
Or maybe giving Him glory in poem
Until the day He calls us Home
What-a-day! What-a-day! A glorious day that will be
When face to face with our Savior we see.

rfoltz 1/2/2012

The Church on the Hill
Beside Stoney Creek

Each day many people pass and wonder why
So many cars; just what happens there?
Uttering, "Glad it's not me" their only reply
It's a church and their time they won't share
With the preachers who only work a day and half each week
At the church on the hill beside Stoney Creek

They are not aware of the Christian School
that teaches children all the subjects
Using the bible as the basic tool
Doing it sincerely without any regrets
It is really more than a day and a half a week
What goes on at the church on the hill beside Stoney Creek

The pastors number three
Serving the needs of one and all
Christianity comes with no charge; it's free
Praying they will stand firm and not fall
While spending much more time then a day and half each week
At the church on the hill beside Stoney Creek

Pastor Chad, the youth pastor
Has a wife and three children who call him "Dad"
At home his family knows him as the master
The youth say he's the best they have ever had
Filling in at least a day and half each week
At the church on the hill beside Stoney Creek

Brother Karl at the Radio Station behind the console
Sending the Christian messages over the air
Trying to reach some poor lost soul
Doing the very best and trying to be fair
While spending his day and a half each week
At the church on the hill beside Stoney Creek

People claim that the Baptist say,
"We are the only ones who are right"
Not knowing they use the Bible as their text
So they will put up a verbal fight
They use God's Word, the Bible; the very best
Getting in his time preaching a day and a half each week
At the church on the hill beside Stoney Creek

They are not concerned about the time they spend
Trying desperately to save some from going to hell
The goal to teach all before the end

At the ringing of that final bell
Knowing their labor is much more than a day and a half each week
At the church on the hill beside Stoney Creek

The church with the skyward-pointing steeple
Facing to the east
Standing tall above the people
Signifying the coming of a wedding feast
There is more than day and a half each week
At the church on the hill beside Stoney Creek

This is Valley Baptist Church by name
Attending each service there are quite a few
Sunday morning and night and Wednesday evening they come
Listening carefully as they sit comfortably in the pew
The pastors know it's more than a day and a half a week
Serving the church on the hill beside Stoney Creek

rfoltz 11/2002

An Easter Message

He "Jesus" Arose

At the trial though innocent of all charges
The gathering crowd's demands came as the largest
Then the sentencing to die on the cross
Little did they know their gain would be their loss

A miracle happened that day
The many were not easy to sway
For in a borrowed tomb He did lay
Sealed with a stone that was rolled away
He went to be with His Father
Those who did not understand, it bothered

Oh, but He did again appear
To the doubting and some had fear
A sad day for all of those
Who did not understand; He arose!

His mission on earth was now complete
Beside His heavenly Father He took His seat
Leaving behind the Holy Spirit for all who believe
It would be a cure for sinful wounds and a great relief

Though He died, He lives!
For the sinner a new life He gives
To those who believe; A Savior for all mankind
At the Lord's table we gather in awe to us remind
The trial, the scourging, humiliation, and suffering He did for us
That all in Him we might find trust

Jesus is to us a most precious name
Knowing Him, we will never be the same
Because some day this sinful world we will no longer roam
That will be when we can call heaven our home

Today He lives as before
And we need Him now more and more
In Him the rejoicing He does bring
With all the hallelujahs we do sing

Easter! What a time to rejoice and give praise
For all He has done in bygone days!

rfoltz 4/13/2009

The Promise of Spring

Though long, cold winter is passing
The chill in the air keeps us guessing
Looking through a cold window pane
The grass is greening; it's not the same
Oh! Then I see a robin or two
Or are my eyes making me a fool?
That means we are sensing another season
A few trees are budding gives another reason
To cheer and shout, "Come on spring!
Come quickly; Do your thing!"

We are looking for the flowers that bloom
And the birds that sing
Warm weather can't get here too soon
With all the beauty it does bring

But there will be grass to mow
Gardens to plow and plant
Thankfully there won't be snow
We must get out and not say we can't

The pleasures that show up
Will cause many aches and pains
Now though winter is completely shut
So from the warmth of summer we have much gain

All need to fall on their knees
Thank God for this time of the year
Offering up to Him our pleas
Giving us a reason to cheer

Spring is here; can summer be far behind?
Get outside and enjoy the weather
To us may it be very kind
To be free as the birds of feather

rfoltz 3/10/2009

Mediator Between God and Man

As I sat in Sunday school one Sunday morn
Now this was before I was reborn
In an effort to make God's Word come alive
The teacher quoted I Timothy chapter 2 verse 5
"There is one mediator between God and man" is what he said
That is Christ Jesus and He's alive; not dead
I spoke up, "There has to be a lawyer or someone to step in"
He replied, "It could only be Jesus to take away our sin"
Not knowing Jesus, I was without a Savior. I was really in the dark
But that woke me up; it set off a spark
It was then I realized I needed to know much more
From A Bible study I learned that it was Jesus
that opened the door
With a desire to know about the Bible, soon I learned its words
are true and because of II Timothy 3:15, 16, & 17, it's also reliable
There are many who may live in a dark world of doubt
By reading the Scripture and listening to the preacher
and Sunday school teacher you can find out
If in His Word we will savor
Soon we will find a satisfying sweet flavor

This could cause you to turn about
With happiness to make you shout
He'll change your life from darkness to light
And do it willingly and quickly without a fight
Come to the altar and on a bended knee
Ask for forgiveness from the heart with a plea
He will do for you what He did for me
Jesus is always ready and willing to mediate
There is no line; you won't have to wait
Being in your pew each Sunday evening and Sunday morn
The Holy Spirit will teach you much more
when you are truly reborn

rfoltz 2/1/2007

What Does the Bible Say?
Check it Out!

When in question about a sin
Get the Bible and check within
The answers are found among the many pages
And has been so throughout the ages
You see, God's Word has never changed
No matter how one tries to rearrange
Hebrews 13:8 makes it clear and clever
He is the same yesterday, today, and forever

By staying in His Word one will always be aware
Of the truth because it is always there
First Corinthians 6:7-11 and Galatians 5:16-21 tell
who will not have eternal life?
Galatians 5:22-26 relates to one who will have no strife

Knowing the Scripture instructs how to face this sinful world
It is a must for all Christian men, women, boys, and girls
When a problem comes about
All will be prepared to stand up and shout

This is what God's Word has to say about that
Why not take time to have a little chat?

Tell them about the Romans Road
Give them a chance to confess to Jesus and unload
All those sinful things of the past
He will take them away and fast

Make sure all we do here on earth
Equals the reward for all it's worth
Check it out and clearly understand
It's in the Bible and a part of God's plan

When one knows for sure
The ungodly way we should not endure
Second Corinthians 17 says come out from among them and separate
But do it now before it's too late

If there is ever a doubt,
Get the Bible and check it out
To be forever in His arms to stay
Follow God's directions; do it His way

This poem could go on and on
One needs to keep in the bible, God's Word
and know to Him you will always belong

Revelation 22:18
For I testify unto every man that heareth the words of the prophecy of this book, If any man shall add unto these things, God shall add unto him the plagues that are written in this book:

rfoltz 6/25/2006

Comfort At Last

Losing a loved one brings us grief
But for Troy, it has brought relief
No more suffering; no more pain
Being with the Lord is forever a gain
Yes, to those left behind
The Lord will comfort them with the passing of time
Let's all give thanks for His heavenly home
In this sin-filled earth He will never more roam
Dwell on what a great reunion that will be
When we all get together up there
Just wait and see
The Lord has promised He will never leave us or forsake us
On this we have God's Holy Word
This we can trust

rfoltz 2/2006

Help is Needed

Hanging in the ushers' closet is a jacket forlorn and lost
Not being used; not worthy of its cost
The owner has up and left it just hanging there
Leaving it all alone with its burden and no one with which to share

If only someone would come and could put it to use
How happy it would be and no longer in abuse
But until the right person comes along
It will just hang there; what a sad song

There is probably no chance of the owner coming back
We will just have to take double duty until we can get
someone to take up the slack
Maybe this guilty one would feel bad
Knowing that his jacket is so very sad

You see we already have one such a person who couldn't care less
He showed us as we put him to the test
Richard M. just wants to get out of it all
And he will give you a lot of jaw

Brother, send out one more plea

We do miss you other than the empty pew

Especially the ushers and, of course, there are others; quite a few

Hope everything is going good as expected to be

All the ushers do miss having you here

But don't feel too bad about us; never fear

All do extend a welcome hand if you can stop in when you are nearby

We'll be as cordial as can be; just give us a try

rfoltz 1/1/2006

The Rain Came Our Way

We have been more than blessed
The Lord knows our needs best
We fret and complain and complain
Just as we think we cannot make it, God sends the rain

Yes, the crops are short and not much to eat
Did you ever think of a diet as a treat?
God knows that we are overweight
We get so hungry we hardly can wait

The sparrows; God feeds them first
None of them will die of thirst
Most of us have too much; more than plenty
We really do not need any

So when the grass is green and there is much
God will supply our need of such and such
Yet we fuss and carry on so
There is enough that we keep on the go

So when there is need

Get on your knees and with the Lord plead

To fill that insufficient amount

Because with the Lord, one can always count

Mathew 5:45b

for he maketh his sun to rise on the evil and on the good,

and sendeth rain on the just and on the unjust.

rfoltz 10/27/2007

Missionaries Everywhere You Look

Look all around you; what do you see?
Pews filled with saints wanting to serve Thee
Missionaries! Missionaries!
Everywhere one can look
Praying to be a servant of this old KJV book
With a heart that is filled with a great desire
To find the worldly wherever they are
And convert them from darkness to light
Even if they want to put up a big fight
Yes, eager to serve the field where God may send
To harvest the fields that are dark with sin
They can be found on all corners of the earth
As a servant of the Lord for all their worth
Let us who have not been called to go
Support these warriors with our prayers and dough
We need to be constantly on our knees
Asking God to answer our pleas
To reward them for their labors of beating the bushes
In satisfying our Lord and Savior with His wishes
All the time we should never forget where we may roam

Our Jerusalem is right here at home

Let's all join in this battle for the lost souls

Making salvation our most important goal

Mark 16:15

And he said unto them, Go ye into all the world,

and preach the gospel to every creature.

rfoltz/6/19/07

Pride Will Take it All

A young man lived in a big house beside the road
Wealthy and influential; he carried his own load
All looked up to him as one they admired
Knowing only what his life required
To the Lord his soul had died
Because of his ego – full of pride

His desires were easily solved
His resources plentiful; with others he rarely became involved
His house was on a long driveway high on a hill
Servants and friends bowed to him at his will
Did they really serve him or did they just abide?
Helping to fill his ego; that awful pride

Wherever he'd go; whatever he'd do
Many folks thought of him as clever and no fool
The fancy automobiles and boats were his desires
Everything was available whatever his heart required
There was little time for family and friends
Just where would this all end?
He'd look down on folks not on his side
Because that ego was filled with pride

In misery and lonely he would finally find out
Too involved, too busy, caused him to start to doubt
With all the things he cherished, did they really satisfy?
What is really needed to just get by?
Sincere friends and family to be at his side
He began to realize to help him with his pride

Learning those around him were really false
Sleep wouldn't come so in bed he'd toss and toss
Questioning himself, "How can I be happy?"
It made him silly and somewhat daffy
He thought and thought; he tried and tried
Was this the real reason, his pride?

His life had just gone from bad to worse
Losing his wife came first
Then out on his own again
Divorce cost those fancy autos, boats, money; now where to begin?
Without friends and family at his side
How could this happen to someone with so much pride?

At his place of employment one day
A devout Christian spoke to him with much to say
Just how to handle the problem that had come his way
In shock, surprised in his tracks he was there to stay
How could this be? He cried and cried
How could I be so troubled with so much pride?

Everything of material wealth was gone
Now how will he carry on?
Decided to take the Christian's advice
Turn it over to the Lord, don't think of it twice
He told him how Christ was born and died
This was the answer to one of such pride

With everything gone, he had lost it all
How could he go wrong, if to the Lord he'd call
They had told him that Jesus Is just a prayer away
Falling on his knees he began to pray
He believed, and Jesus would be at his side
To help him with this terrible pride

Jesus is now carrying that big load
There is no longer a burden of the big house beside the road
Walking daily with Jesus; hand-in hand
Doing the very best, the best he can
Life is now beautiful without all that pride
He now understands why Jesus died

rfoltz 12/30/2005

No One Called His Name

There was a crash on the main highway
Blood, glass, and alcohol ran together that day
However, I did not hear anyone pray
Soon an ambulance came
No one! No, not one heard anyone call upon the Savior's name

Shouting and crying all around could be heard
Of the Lord there was not one word
One driver to the other they laid the blame
Still there was no call on Jesus' name

The injuries were quite severe
Of the Lord not a word one could hear
Alcohol and drugs sounded off loud and clear
Still they argued with one another as they made a claim
Not once did they speak of Jesus' name

Much vulgarity and profanity was continually spoken
God's words were used disrespectfully as a token
Satanic action showed its ugly face
Just how terrible is the human race?

They showed neither remorse nor shame
Neither did they call upon Jesus' name

On the highway lay a body covered in a sheet of white
Not a muscle was moving; there was no more life
One was walking unsteadily and lame
Why, oh why? Did not someone call on Jesus' name?

All of God's adopted children are under His continuous care
Waiting patiently to hear one whisper for the need of prayer
Such a time as this when the accident came
Call before it is too late; let Jesus know you are calling His name

Whether it happens in the day so bright
Or in the darkest of night
It makes no difference what, how, or who
He is waiting; He is never through
What He did for me, He will do for you
Whether it be blame, shame, or just a claim
Since He showed up on earth, He has always been the same
Jesus is there! Always ready and anxious to hear one
calling His name

rfoltz 9/3/2010

Are You Planted by a Well-Watered Stream?

Are you a well-watered tree
Planted by a stream that flows clear and free
With roots near the top of the ground
Where no solid anchor can be found?

There is a Vine that grows forever and ever
Failing not to feed the branches; no never
It reaches down to the bottom of the heart
Where solid growth does start

When anchored as it needs to be
It will never leave or topple and will be strong – that's plain to see
Yes, Jesus is that Vine; great, powerful, and strong
Always wanting others to Him belong

But wait! There are times its branches need to be pruned
Keeping His Word that will come often and soon
A thirst that never satisfies we need to depart
Because Jesus reaches deep down to the heart

It is Jesus that will quench that awful thirst

Don't you want to be first?

It may be later than it may seem

So plant your heart by the ever-flowing stream

Psalm 1:3

And he shall be like a tree planted by the rivers of water, that bringeth forth his fruit in his season; his leaf also shall not wither; and whatsoever he doeth shall prosper.

rfoltz 4/25/2007

Thanksgiving 2001

Once again the time for Thanksgiving
For a beautiful life we are living
The blessings we have are many
God has provided us with plenty

Much food, clothing, and a comfortable home
It's all here; no need to roam
Sharing with family and friends
Our loved one to the very end

We are not in New York City or a foreign land
Or near war-torn Afghanistan
Even though the terrorist cause much fear
Jesus is always very near

As we gather around the Thanksgiving table,
Let us remember those who are not able
To enjoy the blessing the Lord has given to us
All because of Him in whom we put our trust

On this Thanksgiving day; two thousand one

Jesus is still the only one

Ephesians 5:20

Giving thanks always for all things unto God and the Father in the name of our Lord Jesus Christ;

Psalm 26:7

That I may publish with the voice of thanksgiving, and tell of all thy wondrous works.

rfoltz 11/16/2001

Keep Christ in Christmas

Jesus was with God according to John 1:1
He was there when the world begun
Helping in the creation of everything
For service to man; we can shout and sing
He came to earth in a virgin birth to become man
Proving His deity throughout the land

The Church He initiated
Never to be outdated
Coming to answer man's needs
Planting in him the spiritual seeds
Wise men still seek to find Him
Being part of three in one as one of them
Reaching heaven through Him is the only way
Saints rely on Him each and every day

As we already have learned
We await His imminent and soon return
Christ, the only God one can completely trust
Join in and not let them take Christ out of Christmas

rfoltz 12/2003

Scenes like the one above

Speak so clearly of God's love

Oh, how can it be?

That it was so wonderfully prepared for all to see

May the Christmas be bright

Because of Jesus, our guiding light,

And the New Year a most blessed one

Given to us through God's only Son

rfoltz 12/2002

A Task to be Done

Christmas has come and gone
Will you now just linger on
Or will you get busy finding a new resolution?
In the aid of a sinful world's solution?
You've just been refreshed on the birth of God's only Son
That should be enough to encourage us on
Do you need to know the Lord as your Savior?
Which will forever change your behavior
The time has come that the Christian may be put to test
We need to know God's Word and do our best
Let's not let God down
For the answer came in a manger in Bethlehem town
Let's all get busy in the year of two thousand two
That means everyone, including me and you
Stump the bushes and search every nook and cranny
Trying to find the unsaved; we know there are many
So there is a big task to be done
Give all you have to serve Jesus Christ the Son

rfoltz 12/2001

If I Could Only Sing

Oh, if I could only sing
The message I'd bring
Would be, "Let the Joy Bells Ring"
If I did you'd say, "What a ding-a-ling"

With Christmas so near
You can all be of good cheer
I'll not sing or hum, have no fear
I'll just say, "Merry Christmas to all and
I'll pray for you throughout the New Year

rfoltz 12/21/2001

Where is Your Love From?
My Valentine

I'm not Irish, nor am I a Scot

I'm just an old loving German and that's what you got

It makes no difference from where we start

As long as it comes from the heart

When Cupid shot his arrow in my direction,

How happy I was for his selection

Now Cupid is from the imagination

But when our eyes met, Oh, what a sensation

How wonderful, how great, that was just fine

He chose you as my Valentine

Most important about this great love

It came from the Almighty God above

rfoltz 2/14/2003

My 365 Day Valentine

You know not a thing
If you know not how much joy your love does bring
Thankfully, this is not just for today
It's forever, what more can I say?
It was because of you the Lord came to know us
Together we learned in whom to put our trust
He taught us how to love one another
And to serve Him like a brother
You're always there ready, willing, and able
To help me all the time
365 days each year, you are my valentine

rfoltz 2/14/2004

Christmas Eve Night

It was Christmas eve, what was the matter?
Waiting and listening I could hear no clatter
I threw up the window and peered into the night
The moon was big, beautiful, and casting much light
But not a reindeer was in sight
There was no new fallen snow
Hardly any traffic, and it was traveling very slow

Opening the Bible I saw the trouble
One that nearly burst my bubble
God's Word doesn't mention a Christmas like this
He has a very different Christmas list
Reading and reading I didn't fall asleep
Being interested in Jesus birth,
I didn't utter a peep
Being born in Bethlehem town
In the Inn no room could be found
He was laid in a manger
From Herod, soon would come a danger
Who thought the King of Kings would threaten his throne
Afraid he would have no crown of his own.

Wise men came from the east
To see the only one who could bring peace
Three kings came from afar
All following the light of a star
Giving gifts only fit for the King of Kings
And for a Savior with the news it brings
Performing many miracles, healing the sick,
Causing the blind to see as He went about
Healing the lame at the pool causing him to cry out
Zacchaeus climbed to a tree top so he could see
Jesus said, "Come, I must stay with thee"
He gave him salvation which was free

Jesus, He went preaching and praying as Christians should
Converting all that He could
As a Savior to the world, a world that was lost
For this He hung on a cross
Through this came salvation He offered it to you and me
Lasting forever and throughout all eternity
Finding the true reason for a special night
I went peacefully to bed saying
"Merry Christmas to all and to all, Good night"

rfoltz 10/27/2001

Pastor Bailey
Thanks for 30 Years

You have shared with us for these past 30 years
Humbly and graciously; God's Word without fear
You preached and taught the Bible with your convictions
To serve God faithfully, truthfully, consistently with His restrictions
Though there were times of ups and downs
Continually you served Him without a frown
There were times of challenge, of disappointment and health
Still from the Scriptures came the encouragement of spiritual wealth
We have gathered to fellowship in honor of your dedicated service to one and all
Most importantly for us, you answered God's call
What a wonderful day that will be on the streets of gold
When all you have ministered to will gather, the number untold
Again, we are most grateful for your dedicated service here at Valley Baptist Church
Because you have always put this ministry first
Through you we have learned of God's great love

And how it enters into our hearts through Jesus and
the God above
We look forward to many more years of your preaching
And to all in our Jerusalem you will be reaching
Let us continue to walk hand in hand
Here in the Shenandoah Valley converting all we can

rfoltz 2/19/2009

After Thoughts; Bits and Pieces

Bits and pieces gathered throughout the ages
Read them and ask, "Do I fit among these pages?
Am I one of these?
If so, help me outgrow them please!

Growing old with much experience of the past
Qualifies one to answer questions frequently asked.
Having lived through the ups and downs, the ins and outs of many
Highs and lows
Gives us reason to know how life really goes.

To pass on from the "Literary College
Bits and Pieces of Useful Knowledge".

rfoltz/ 2/15/2011

From the light of the cross

Jesus makes the difference
When we fell on our knees
Crying out to Jesus, "Forgive us of our sins, please!"
Hearing our request, He set us free
The reason He died on that cruel, old tree.
Each Sunday we enter into an open church door
Seeking to learn of His Word more and more.
From the world of sin to one of pure light
Heaven will now be our home with great delight

Valley Baptist Church

The Lighthouse Sends a Gleam

The Lighthouse sends its gleam through the land
Praying it will enter each and every man.
Teaching to the heart as none others do
That it may fall on the open minds of me and you.

The times goes all too fast
For us of the Lighthouse class.
But with our focus on the teaching, we learn so much
Both young and old are taught as such.
Being instructed from the old King James
You so carefully pronounce those Biblical names.
Teaching book by book and verse by verse
With time for comments or just converse.

The young learn of what, how, and whom to teach
That God's Word will have an outreach.
They have so much ahead of them
They can teach their children and others without a whim.
We who are elderly learn from the heart
Somehow we qualify as "too soon old and too late smart".

Some learn, while others get trampled about the toes
Whatever the consequence, that is just how it goes.
We sit under the Lighthouse that gives much praise
Here at Valley Baptist, you, brother Fauver, are that
Lighthouse who instructs us to have better and more blessed days.

Sunday after Sunday, you send out that gleam
Praying that the Holy Spirit will cause many to come clean.
Someday when we join together on the streets of gold,
All can say this is what you taught, "I told you so".

rfoltz 2/8/2011

A Bully meets His Match

Walking home from school all alone
The bully hurled snide remarks at me
I answered, "Sticks and stones may break my bones
Your rudeness will not hurt you see.
There is one bigger than the two of us
Even though you may want to make a fuss."

It matters not how big and strong
There is one who walks close by me
The one to whom I belong
Raise your hand in threat and you'll see
And learn just how this can be.

It was then that I asked him to take a look
Of a most intriguing and informative book
He stood in question and awe
Thinking, "I'm about to have a ball!"
He said, "Into the unknown I'm being led
No little sassy girl will ever lead me astray
That would be some great day."

Little did he know of the power this book has
He was saying, "That's a bunch of jazz."
All the time the Spirit of the Lord was setting him up
Little did he know he'd be drinking from a cup.
That continues to overflow with blessings from above
To shower him with overflowing love.

Telling him this is a story that will fill his heart
The book of John is a good place to start.
Keep reading; reading to learn how it will end
All the time you will be developing a new friend.
Be sure to read the book of Revelation
'Cause now you have reached the ultimate goal of salvation.

Now that you have learned so very much
You can quit bullying because there is
A new one to whom you can clutch.
No longer are you the same as before
Being a child of God you are much, much more.
Knowing and loving you has changed my life
So much so I want you to be my wife.

This could be the end of the story if there wasn't more to tell

You see my bullying brought on a different direction to keep me out of hell.

The Lord Jesus has brought me from darkness to the True Light

It was so very easy and with no fight.

I've been blessed you took the time to show me the way

Because Jesus took me in and is keeping me forever in His arms to stay.

rfoltz 3/15/2011

"Thou Shalt Not!"

God called on Moses, "Come up here"
These are words every man, woman, and child should hear.
"Thou shalt not"
This should always be remembered and not forgot
The Ten Commandments are to rule all throughout the land
Christians should quote them and take a firm stand.
"Thou shalt not have any other gods"
throughout the land where man has ever trod.
Thou shalt not worship any images like the God the love
Coming in place of the almighty from the heavens above.
Thou shalt not take His name in vain
Remember! The tongue is a hard thing to tame.
Keep the Sabbath holy in time for worship and prayer
God is listening; He's everywhere!
Honor your father and mother
They are the only ones; there will never be another.
Thou shalt not murder, commit adultery, steal
Or bear false witness; it is His will.
Thou shalt not covet thy neighbor's house, his wife,
Nor his male or female servants, nor his ox, donkey, or anything

Because of the suffering and pain it may bring.

Don't say, "Oh! I forgot"

And get disobedient to the "Thou shalt not's"

Don't try to give our God a test

He has already promised to give us His very best.

The Ten Commandments are His "forget me nots"

As well as His "Thou shalt not".

Rfoltz 3/20/2011

Section II

OUR COUNTRY

Our country stands proud and salutes the flag and what it stands for: The freedoms and rights to worship as one desires.

Give thanks daily through prayer.

A Judgment Day is Coming

From coast to coast
Our nation has lost much of what to boast
Suffering from moral decay
What would our forefathers say?
From Massachusetts to New York and California
They permit same-sex marriages
While in Alabama the courts performed a social miscarriage
What has become of justice for all?
The ACLU has turned it into a courtroom ball
If revival would break out, and we'd repent and turn around,
A new life would soon abound
While reading between these lines,
God's Word surely makes clear and it defines
The way the world should travel
A new direction would soon unravel
Rather it be same-sex marriages or the Ten
Commandments taken out
God's Word leaves for the Christian no room for doubt

As we ponder, nationally, these points
Keep cool, don't get upset or out of joint
Stand erect and tall; don't squirm
Take the Scriptures without exception; be firm
The Ten Commandments are the basis for all laws
Study them and learn; they are without flaws
Let all Christians stand up and be heard
We wholly believe the truth is revealed in God's Word
God will have the final say
Judgment is coming. It could be today

rfoltz 2/2004

Better Days Ahead?

Each year comes with many ups and downs
Bringing much happiness laced with frowns
The passing of loved ones and friends
Things we remember as the year ends

Among the births, weddings, reunions, all good times,
Then came tragedies, dark days with no reason or rhymes
The threat of terrorism sure does try the patience
Of what was once called a "free nation"

As the first year of the century comes to an end
Let us not forget why this nation began
May we wisely use these experiences as a tool
Praying there will be brighter days in two thousand two

rfoltz 10/22/2001

I Shed a Tear This Memorial Day

This morning as Ron sang "America",
Tears came into my eyes
I remember some friends who gave their lives
I was thirteen on that December 7, 1941
Not old enough a uniform I could don
Just who would be called to go fight?
Whoever would go, it would not be a delight
Would it be my brother or my Dad?
These were frighten fears that I had
Would I have to take care of Mom and me?
There were three of us you see
Because of age and a family
My Dad was deferred; we rejoiced happily
But my brother had to go
I really missed him; that cannot go untold
And a lot of my friends got the call
James, Herman, and Billy, and that's not all
But these three a supreme sacrifice they made
A world war sent them to the grave
By now I had fast become of age

To help with the war in which we were engaged
So many gave their lives that we may be free
Let me make a very solemn plea
When you gather to worship and pray,
Be thankful for the good, old USA
Most important of all,
Be ready, willing, and able to answer the call
That's about all I have to say
As we celebrate this Memorial Day

rfoltz 5/2001

Flag Day

June 14th is Flag Day
Beautiful colors for the USA
Yes, the red, white, and blue
Provided much for me and you

Raise it high on its staff
While some may ridicule and others laugh
Most know what it stands for
For many it has opened wide a door

Many have crossed the boarders by chance
Just to change their circumstance
Because they really know
What it offers and has to show

As Old Glory waves on high
Still some really wonder why
All the wars have been fought
Not realizing what has been bought

Look around and see
Just what it has done for the family
There is freedom plus plenty
No lack for needs, no not any

The freedom to pray on bended knees
Go to the Lord with our pleas
Please remember to the God above
We'd have nothing without his love

rfoltz 5/2001

A Tribute to Memorial Day

Many will gather to give praise and honor to the fallen
Who have given and proudly served as their calling
On the battlefields they bravely fought a good fight
For even those who opposed who didn't see the light
As a memorial to a nation that is so great
Remembering the past, the present and to the future relate
It was for a democracy; the freedom for everyone
So that the rights and justice could be properly done
Let us stand erect and salute the flag of freedom of the USA
Standing at attention and salute the Christian flag and pray
It will be done through Jesus Christ to do it God's way

rfoltz 5/28/2005

A Patriotic Tree

A patriotic tree; American through and through
All decorated in red, white, and blue
Lights that fade in and out
Reminds us of a democracy with a lot of clout
Violently they flash on and off
Bringing attention to the many wars that have been fought
The red bows speak loud of those who shed their blood
As the eagle spreads his wings over the remains of a flood
Stars recall the country we love
Given to us from God above
Counting our blessings is a must
Because God gave a nation we can trust
Remembering the 9/11 attack
Stirred patriotism where there was a lack
Memories will linger on of nine eleven
Leaving us with the thoughts of heaven
This great nation USA
Is worth fighting for any day
While gathering around the patriotic tree
Praying this land will always remain free

rfoltz 12/2001

Sergeant Woods

Though our paths have never crossed
We feel it is our loss
To never have met one as brave as you
Means you are a true hero for what you do

At a time when our nation is in a turmoil
Over rather we should be fighting on foreign soil
Battles are different that we now fight
But we are proud of those that serve for this
God-given right

Though it may be in an area of sand and oh, so hot!
It is sure necessary to protect our land like it or not
Your sacrifice has made us so very sad
To be in harm's way because of the leaders of Baghdad

Your "Dad" of you is mighty proud
To us at church he would sound off clear and loud
Every so often he'd give us a "Bunky Report"
Rather it is in a foreign service or here in an army fort.

You see we attend church together
Praying that you will be completely healed and better
My wife and I join in with a most sincere gratitude
That your service to the USA was with a servant's attitude

Yes, we remember you in each and every day
When we go to the Lord and pray
Though you may be injured and not able to get around
Comfort is in the Lord; where peace can be found

rfoltz 9/8/2006

Korea, What Was It?

June 1950 in Korea they started a war
Many are still asking, "Just what for?"
They could not even give it a name
Calling it "a police action" or "a conflict"; it's all the same
When men go to the battlefield on different side
Lined up against each other with guns blazing, following orders
"men died"!
Thousands killed, thousands upon thousands wounded
and prisoners taken and 8,000 still missing
"War is not the name!", they keep insisting
Planes bombed, big guns fired as the Chinese poured over the Yalu River
A might blow to our forces they did deliver
The commander was fired; they wouldn't let him do his job
All the rounds shot, bombs were dropped, and the mortars were lobbed

Where was the strength of this little nation from?
Being able to get to the source was not to come
This action lasted three years and a bit

When after a fashion, they decided to quit
Was this political or communism threat?
Either one could be true, my life I'd bet
It's now been 50 years, and I still don't understand
What was this in this foreign land?
Life, liberty, peace, and the pursuit of happiness is what
we fight for
So why didn't they just call it war?
Now with all said and done
Who really won?

rfoltz 7/2003

PS: Since around the world so many wars have been fought
Without once giving our Creator a thought
If only this nation would turn from its sinful ways and repent
God would more than bless this land for every life
that has been spent

Awakening Call

Wake up America, answer the call
A warning has been sent to one and all
Out of the heavens planes seem to fall
Bringing a time of great devastation
Upon what was founded as a Christian nation
A nation so full of sin
Is this how God will begin?
Let's recognize it before it's too late
Or will this be America's fate?
Fall to your knees and humbly pray
Asking forgiveness, do it today

rfoltz 9/2001

Our Nation in Need

In our nation's capitol, Washington DC
Congress makes laws concerning you and me
These folks sure seem to believe
OF all these rules they are relieved
The news reports a lot of misbehaving
In our nation's capitol there is a haven

They have taken prayer and God's Word out of school
This creates what the Bible calls a fool
Another decision they made
Was concerning "Roe vs Wade"
Why doesn't congress recognize the flaw?
In our nation's capitol, we're backed against the wall

Many of these are far from home
They take the liberty to stray and roam
To many of them this is their downfall
Not answering their constituents call
In our nation's capitol, the Congressional Hall

They seem to have forgotten the reason they are there
It is not to see how well they fare
We would like them to see the signs
According to Scripture we're nearing the end times
Our nation's capitol is falling further behind

Yes, they took God's Word out of schools
The Ten Commandments off the walls;
just who are they trying to fool?
We need people who stand and shout
If you want to mistreat our nation, then get out!

We need those who will take a stand and fight
For everything to be just and right
Let them be rid of corruption and be reliable
Let them rule our nation according to the Bible

rfoltz 7/2001

A Threat With a Defense

A threat with Anthrax
Sure has an essence of a terrorist attack
They are trying to fill us with a fear
Deprive us a freedom we hold so dear
And will continue to do so year after year
Trying to tear us morally down
Till not one Christian can be found
Or take away all our wealth
And destroy our health
They claim to be Godly folks
To the Christian they are a big joke
The terrorist are a cowardly bunch
That's a fact and not just a hunch
The Christian has the perfect antidote
Answers are in the Bible, and we can quote
Jesus came as a Savior for all who will accept Him
He'll give us the strength to face up to them
The Lord could be giving us a warning
Soon He'll be returning for the saints some beautiful morning
Don't let the terrorist lay on you a threat
Accepting the Lord Jesus is the best defense one can get.

rfoltz 11/2001

From a Vet of Old to a Vet So Bold

I tried and tried to write you a poem
Words wouldn't come until I witnessed you coming home
Then they came, they stared to roll
Words that may help calm the soul
Jessica, as you and Greg rode in the parade
An example of America you two made
There is no country in the world where I would rather be
Than the good old US of A; the land of the free
Having noble soldiers to go and fight for freedom, liberty, and peace
Gives one and all in life a new lease
The "507th" will be happy you made it through
Proudly saluting that you were willing to fight for the Red, White, and Blue
I never got a bronze star or a purple heart
That has been more than fifty years ago
When I was young and brave with patriotism to show
Knowing that in the hospital you laid
Praying for complete recovery to be made
Jessica and Greg, we have never met
I gratefully and honorably call you a fellow vet

rfoltz 7/23/2003

9/11/01

New York, USA

September eleventh, two thousand one,
A very dark valley in New York had begun
Terrorist made an aerial attack
In expertise there was no lack
The 110 story World Trade Center they did bring down
Many lives were lost and the missing are to be found
It's being compared to the Pearl Harbor bombing of years ago
Bringing our nation to a new low
Remembering by the dawn's early light
Suddenly the future doesn't look very bright
Surviving the Civil War the nation was brought together
Facing many crises, the USA seems to weather
WWI, WWII, Korea, Vietnam, the Cold War, and Desert Storm
brought about a new challenge
Keeping us busy there was no time to lounge
Was it through the time of peace
We left our guard down? Never expecting times such as these
You see, this country needs to awake
From the sinful way it did take

God must come back on the scene
For all the acts of disobedience He has seen
Our leaders need to give us someone to look up to
Many in government have acted such a fool
Let us fall to our knees
And pray to God this nation turn around, please
So as the Lord prepares for us a mansion in heaven
Let us all remember, 2001 on nine eleven
May we not forget that dark day
And what took place in New York, USA

rfoltz 9/2001

It's Worth it All

From the American Revolutionary War to Iraq
and now Afghanistan
Many a brave and courageous one took a stand
To give to "America the Beautiful" their very best
Those whom may follow will have the pursuit of happiness,
life, and liberty without a contest
Oh so many went to the grave
Hoping and praying that those behind could be saved
Praying for all who are sentenced to a wheelchair
While in their hearts they show them they really care

Bunky, hardly a day goes by that we don't think of you
Praying for a miracle that would make you like new
With an attitude that is beyond belief
Though suffering as you must, hopefully God will give you relief
Thank you from the bottom of my heart for your service to this
great nation
No country in the world can say to their citizens they have these
outstanding relations
Yes, America is beautiful, the best on this planet earth
All the brave, young men and women who have
sacrificed give it its worth.

rfoltz 8/28/2009

Proud to Be an American, But I Shed a Tear

Sitting in a most comfortable pew; gazing at our nation's flag
To be an American, I'm mighty glad
It was Sunday before the Memorial Day celebration
A time when we remember those giving their lives for this great nation
The preacher started his sermon, and I sat in my pew
Suddenly realizing the church was decorated in red, white, and blue
The flowers of the same hue surrounded the area of the pulpit
The communion table held an old flag and a bugle that had been used quite a bit
The preacher continued his sermon, but my mind wandered away
Remembering the past wars fought that we could celebrate this Memorial Day
Comfortably sitting there with freedom and without fear
My eyes welled up with a tear

Studying the flag with all its glory and beauty
These brilliant colors that called many to their duty

Stripe of white reminds one of the purity it represents
Red a color of blood that so many brave souls spent
A field of royal blue; how richly it stands
Fifty stars represent the states that unite to protect this blessed land
From around the world they come just to be near
The flag that offers freedom and protection; they'll shed a tear

Wait, let's be reminded how this came all about
It will be then we'll say, "Hallelujah" and shout
Our founding fathers saw a real need
To worship according to their convictions and to plant a seed
God brought them to establish a land that would be free
As they had come from far over
To inaugurate a government not for only one but for all
And unite the states that would not fall
Each and everyone would hold in their hearts freedom to worship the Lord they love very dear
Though they may have to suffer as they shed a tear

These colors, bright and cheerful, wave so gallantly the red, white, and blue
Stands confirming a word we know is true
The Bible, God's Word men of old penned it down

The Narrow Way Home

A new land the Pilgrims God directed to be found
A place where these folks could give glory to God
and worship as they will
Nowhere on earth could be better than this; their needs to fulfill
Now they could their Lord and Savior worship without fear
For this rejoicing they shed a tear

As the preacher preached, he gave us what
the Lord laid on his heart
God through Jesus Christ is the place to start
These colors begin with the white
The purity from God is sure a delight
Red is for the shedding of blood through Jesus, His son
Freely offering salvation to each and everyone
Blue is for the royalty of god who stand alone and above all
To those in obedience and willing to answer the call
Stars beckon the Christian from all corners of the earth
To come together, stand up and fight for God with all their worth
Above the stars will be our God-given eternal home
By God's grace and mercies we will no longer have
this wicked world to roam
Yes to be an American I'm surely glad
To stand proud and salute the grand old flag
But I still can't help wondering why
We've been so blessed as we celebrate the 4th of July

Now in these waning years
Bring about to this nation aspirations with trembling fear
One cannot help shedding a tear

John 11:35

Jesus wept.

rfoltz 6/17/2003

The Grand Ole Flag

Gazing upon the grand ole flag
I'm proud to be an American, I like to brag
There is much to be seen through these brilliant colors
Much cannot be said of many others

Yes, looking at the stripes of red
Reminds me of the battlefields where many have bled
They died waging a great fight
For the purity represented by the stripes of white

Pointing to the fifty stars that have come together
Of the many storms we have weathered
Mounted on a field of royal blue
Offering freedom to every race, color, or creed; including me and you

A president once said, "Don't ask what you country can do for you; but what you can do for it"
The answer should be, continue to serve her and never quit

Another president on the way to Gettysburg said, "It will not be
long remembered what was said or done here"
You see, they fought for freedom without a fear
Doesn't that instill a want to cheer?

Those beautiful colors one witnesses as they wave on high
Or as they gallantly pass by
Proudly stand
Stand erect, covering your heart with your hand
Saluting the flag of this great land
Proud and brave we should willingly brag
To be able to serve
The grand ole flag

rfoltz 8/2003

From Less to More in 2004

The headline news of the year
Instilled in many a new fear
Yes, 2003 went by very quickly
Suddenly the flu hit and many became sickly
February saw space shuttle Columbia in mid-air disintegrate
For any rescue it was much too late
Kidnapping of Elizabeth Smart
Hurricane Isabel caused much destruction before she did impart
Iraq elected to enter war
Rather than surrender to forces from afar
Threats came boldly from Saddam
Until finally he was overcome
Murders, California fires along with many other disasters
How could so much happen and could it come any faster?
California voters, the governor they did recall
Strange things happen in politics
Not much changed, they are still up to their old tricks
Democratic presidential candidates there must be nine or ten
So many, one does not know where to begin
John Muhammad and Lee Malvo, the snipers had their day in court and were tried

Muhammed got death and Malvo got life in prison, but he never cried
Oh, the terrorists brought types of threat
One that would be the greatest yet
If there was not enough with all of these,
Along came the mad cow disease
Now the church is being attacked by the homosexual crowd
God says this is an abomination, it's just not allowed
To top it off, the Ten Commandments were taken to the test
Satan continues to do his best to bring to God contempt
We know that God will defeat Satan in his evil attempt
Whatever may stand out in your mind of the year 2003,
Remember God's children whom He has set free
Christians stand up; be counted because with God, we're great
Do it now before it's too late
Let us be thankful for all the blessings in 2003 we had
We've been delivered from much of the evil and the bad
Pray He'll show us the way to open the door
That many souls can know for sure
The true way to heaven as always before
From less to more; let that be your goal for 2004

rfoltz 12/2003

God, Family, and Country

God made it this way right from the beginning
The Bible tells us God made everything; the heaven and earth
Right down to Revelation, the ending
Of Adam and Eve and all their worth.

After the Creation, then came Adam
From a rib He made Eve
A fallen angel named Satan
Causing Adam and Eve to be deceived
By eating of the apple thus the beginning of sin.

There they gave birth to Cain and Abel
The start of the family
They now had two more to set at the table.
As a witness and would be more for the world to see.

God's Word says He is a jealous God
He wants no other god to try to take His place
Or to lay claim to even a little piece of His sod
Of anyone in an area where He can trace.

As a father and mother who are to raise their child
As the Bible teaches
The Bible makes it all worthwhile
If into their heart that it reaches.

When they are old, they will not depart from it
If when they are young, they may stray
Have patience; they will return and not quit
And God will accept never again to go astray.

rfoltz 9/20/2010

A Final Farewell; Chalmers

Though the Lord let us give proof
That as younglings we could not raise the roof
But we did make a place in life
By letting each of us find a wife.

Chalmers you made a career in the US Navy
Which turned out to be your gravy
Giving the country 22 good years
Stood tall, proudly serving without fears.

Though suffering ~~may~~ MANY aches and pains
But was outstanding in all of your gains
You served your employers with pleasure
Giving them plenty and a gainful measure.

Your family you provided for quite well
Outliving your wife with whom many years you did dwell.
Mike and Jeff, your two boys
In your final days brought you much joy.

In the service to humanity, you gave your best
From us left behind give you an "A" plus, you passed the test.

Remembering "the good ole school days"
We were young and things were different in many ways
The passing of time has changed us all
Not allowing us the ability to have a big final ball.

Now the time has come when the "Rough & Ready Guys"
Are older and surely wiser
Gathering to say "FAREWELL" and to reduce our size
We are now just two with hindered lives.

Chalmers; "MY BEST FRIEND"
"I hoped they would never end!"
With tears flowing and a SADDENED HEART
It's mighty hard to say GOODBYE and DEPART!
"Let me give you a final SALUTE"
My "Ole Buddy, Pal, and Friend"
Until someday when we'll meet again.
You have split us three and made us two
HOWEVER WE WILL GO ON
FOREVER REMEMBERING YOU!

rfoltz 6/9/2012

A Fair Weather Christian

Awaking this morning to see the ground covered with snow
Quickly I said, "We'll not go out to brave the cold!"
We'll stay home and listen to the radio WOTC
In the comforts of our home we hope to hear what
the Preacher has today for you and me.

It's Sunday! A Church Day for all Christians here below
But the pews, there will be a few no – shows
Our get-up and go doesn't want to get up and go
That happens when one gets old.

To the Lord, we will ask for His forgiveness for not making this trip
Though we will get into His word via radio we'll dip
For us "The Fair Weather Christian" we don't
want to be left behind
However, to us it does make a difference if the SUN does shine
PLEASE FORGIVE US IF WE ARE NOT THERE
SUNDAY AM, SUNDAY OR WEDNESDAY NIGHT
AS FAIR WEATHER CHRISTIANS LORD,
PLEASE! KEEP US ALWAYS IN SIGHT!
GOD'S WORD TO US IS ALWAYS A DELIGHT!

rfoltz 2/17/2013

Section III

WE GIVE PRAISE

To those who serve and live in obedience to God,
through His Son who gave us His all, we give praise

A Close-up
of
The Many Faces of
a
"COUNTRY BOY"

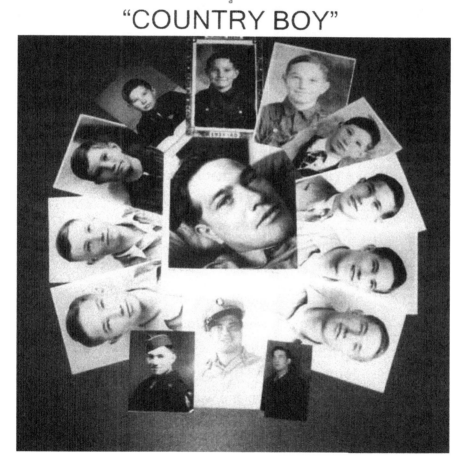

That's How God Works

For many years I wouldn't or couldn't have cared less
Knowing of Jesus or why He died
That was when I walked in vanity and with worldly pride
Realizing the errors of my ways, I bowed my head and cried.

"Please forgive me for all my evil and sinful ways"
Was the reason I finally prayed
All the many faces that I have shown
Not ever having any idea or known
That my youth was so sinfully spent
And that is the way it always went.

A disobedient and worldly life that I had
Must have made God sad
He knew that I was lost
He informed me that "He is our Heavenly BOSS"
I finally accepted Him and was relieved to know
I'm now Heaven bound!
And those sins can now "nowhere be found".
They are gone as far as the east is from the west
Oh How Thankful I am that I passed the test.

To God I'm so deeply indebted!
He gets the Glory and all the credit
Yes! for all those unrighteous years I traveled the land,
I was quite a Jerk!
God so quickly forgave me! "THAT'S HOW HE WORKS".

rfoltz 3/8/2014

Pastor Chad Preached a Sermon on Turning Aside

On the back side of the desert Moses was trying to hide
When a burning bush he spied,
Not being consumed a closer look he tried
No, this is holy ground! God cried
The Lord called Moses, he answered, "Here am I"
It was there he turned aside
As God spoke, Moses hid his face; he shied
He received instruction that was to be applied
Aaron spoke to him; he lacked eloquence. He swallowed his pride
Forty years through the wilderness he led Israel to the mountainside
A fire at night and cloud by day; on God he relied
He was faithful, not along just for the ride
Water, food, and clothing God continually supplied
Spying out the "Promised Land", two said, "yes" and the others lied
Not entering the land of milk and honey he died
He is now a part of the heavenly bride
Because of his obedience by turning aside

rfoltz 4/2003

Rose, We care

Rose – Rose, we really do care
A little tidbit we want to share
When we call upon you; you are always there
With your knowledge, ability, and willingness we often have a need
To you we make a plead
Your cooperation with a smile completes the deed

Oh, sometimes it seems we are going to fight
But really neither of us is uptight
Even if sometimes our request seems out of line
You never act as though you do mind

From the bottom of our hearts (yes we have one) you do touch
For this we want to thank you very much

rfoltz 9/8/10

PS You may think this is the end
It isn't, I just might begin

Bet you never thought you would make my book of poems
I've saved many spaces as my mind may want to roam
(no comments please)
To give to you the praise you deserve
No, that took no amount of nerve
Because we know the Lord does bless you
For all the kind deeds you do
This is really the end; there is no more
I'm closed down and shut the door
I do want to help make your day
What else could I do or say?

"Son Rise"
by Max Sheets

"As you lie in The Morning Hour
Searching for The Perfect Thought
"The Beast Seeks To Devour
Before First Light is Draught

"Aware of The Redeemer
And His Amazing Grace
Makes That Darkness step down
And The "Son's" Light takes its place.

Beryl, Looking for You Back

We hear you are feeling kind of poorly
That's better than being worldly
The doctors are probing inside and out
Trying with all their might to find the problem without a doubt
Now we don't pray to the "man upstairs"
But we are asking God to give them the answer; that's our prayers
We are sure looking to see you in your pew
'Cause you are missed by quite a few
Please get better. We need you in the kitchen
All we men want breakfast; we are itchin'
To see your bright and smiling face
The first Saturday of each month in your place
We're aware of your being so good looking
But it's really your good cooking
So you see we don't want you sick
"Cause you are really needed and quick

rfoltz 9/24/2009

The Man of the Hour
Our Neighbor

Going to the window and looking out
Seeing a neighborly gesture, there was no doubt
A man and his daughter from around my car shoveling snow
Tears welled up and began to flow
Having had a heart attack and now asthma, I'm handicapped
In a weakened condition my energy is somewhat sapped

But this man, somewhat elderly, is a retired preacher
Now serving the Lord as a Sunday school teacher
He hasn't forgotten; he still practices what he preaches
As far out as his word reaches
In heaven there will be rewards a plenty
Not just a few, but many
Practicing his Christianity he's sincere. He really cares
You see, he's our neighbor who lives upstairs
May God bless and keep you for being the neighbor you are
In our case you've been the man of the hour

rfoltz 2/2004

Brother Ed, regardless of what others may say, I think you are tops; especially on that snowy day.

To Patsy and Boys

We share with you in this great loss
Remember, the Lord has called, and He is the boss
Though it is a time for you to be sad,
You can look toward heaven and be glad
Knowing that it is also a time to be bold
Because now your loved one walks the streets of gold
Even though you know how much he will be missed,
Jesus has made provisions for such a time as this
It is His love for you on how He does care
For He has promised you will be able to join him up there
Jayne and I have not seen you for awhile
But remember our talks with a smile
Now you will be in our prayers more
As things will not be the same as before
It is the love of Jesus we will remain,

Randolph & Jayne

The Inbodens

There is a Dad, Larry, and son, Terry
This is enough to squash any worry
Then there is Matthew, Andrew, and Mark
This is surely, definitely no lark
Only God could give a mother five so Godly men
It does not happen often; I know not when

What a wonderful world this would be
If everyone could have such a blessed family
The testimony of this family has been revealed
There seems to be no room for an appeal
Only from a world so steeped in sin
Could a challenge ever begin

Thank you so very much for the impression on us you have made
There is nothing in this world would I ever trade
For the walk with God that is so impressive to all
Praying always there will never be a fall

How could one ever forget Barbara who in this had a big hand?

As a wife, mother, a Proverbs 31, she takes a stand

We continue to ask the Lord each and every day

That your testimony would only get better as we pray

rfoltz 4/9/2008

The Lord Gave a Call
Daniel Answered

Here am I Lord, send me
Not knowing where it would be
After college it was Russia first
Where missions became your thirst
Then off to China you would go
Maybe it would be here; you did not know

Spending a year and half there
This is it! Now with the mission board you must share
Being accepted, now would come deputation
A very new and different situation
Then all the support needed was raised
To God be the glory along with praise

Oh, ordination was yet to take place
A committee of preachers you'd have to face
Could this cause one to be nervous?
No, for to God will be this service
Passed the test, and it is now behind you

The charge was given of what you are to do
A celebration at Valley Baptist with family and friends a fellowship
The near final preparation for the big trip

Now in China where you found the joy of your life
The one who will soon be your wife
But wait, there will be more school
To learn the language and with the Bible as your tool
Though from home a half a world away,
Distance makes no difference when we pray
Prayers will come from us, one and all
Elated, proud, and happy that you answered the call

rfoltz 2/3/2004

To Mrs. Keziah
Delivering Cheer

We come to present to you this poem
From our place to your home
We are not wise men from the east
Moreover we are not riding a beast
We are not three kings led by a star
We don't even come from afar
We are relaying the Good News
That was once given to the Jews
We bring you good tidings with lots of cheer
As we celebrate our Lord and Savior again this year
Please accept this token of love
With blessings that come from the God above
From the 5th and 6th grades of the Valley Baptist Christian School
A very Merry Christmas and Happy New Year; especially to you

rfoltz 12/ 2001

A Mean Man With His Sword

There is a man so very mean
He's not big in stature and quite lean
His Sword, the Bible in hand
Travels all over this land
Meeting a sinner he comes down rough
With his Sword hidden in his heart, he can be tough
Yes, he's really a mean man
Serving the Lord the best he can
He will drive a long way out and back
Just to pass out a few tracts
He can put up a big bout
'Cause he and the Sword carry much clout
There just isn't one so mean
To bring a sinner to Jesus on whom he can lean
With his Sword hidden in his heart
He'll set a convert off to a right start
Don't believe he can make a fist
But what he tells you, you can believe this
He can tell a sinner how to come clean
He's rough and tough with a heart full of love

Sent to him from God on the wings of a dove
Now if you see him coming, stand your ground
Not a better Christian can be found
He says he's as mean as a junkyard dog
No one knows the miles for the Lord he has logged
This mean man is always on the look
To share with someone from his Sword, the Bible, the Great Book

rfoltz 11/2001

Now Ivor is his name
He just makes you happy he came
Of God's Word he is never ashamed

A Gracious Lady

My mother-in-law, a gracious lady was she
One who knew the pangs of poverty
A beautiful young lass
Who desired to be upper class
Struggling to raise young ladies three
To share with men who will agree
No one could have done better even with a degree
Intellectual and humble, one with lots of charm
Concern for all caused her much alarm
The growing up with convictions of old
Always willing to dispense advice, she was bold
To know her surely was much pleasure
What she had to offer could never be measured
Words of wisdom she would often write down
Tucking them away in a book or the Bible to be later found
Sharing with me I'm a most grateful one
Because the ear of my mother-in-law I had won
To her I want to say many, many thanks
The legacy she left her family is better than money in the banks

So to you, Maryanna, I dedicate this poem

For someday soon we will share heaven as our home

rfoltz 7/13/2001

Proverbs 3:5 & 6

Trust in the LORD with all thine heart;

and lean not unto thine own understanding.

In all thy ways acknowledge him, and he shall direct thy paths.

Fifteen Years Later

As now I reminisce
Oh, how our conversations I do miss
The discussions of many things we had
Both of the good and the bad
Often Bible passages we would discuss
Knowing God's Word we could always trust
In these topics we came on a common ground
Because in the Bible the answers could be found

How I remember the night in the hospital you said,
""Why doesn't God take me home instead?"
I answered, "God is not through with you yet
There will be more witnessing, you can bet."
The very next day your neighbor came
Yes, Mrs. Neil was there to see you just the same
It was then you asked her about her salvation
I do not know her answer on her relation
I do know that night to you, God made the call
Into His loving arms you did fall

rfoltz 9/14/2010

The 6'6" Evangelist

To you, Brother Tozer, a long tall drink of water is what you are
Filled with the Living Water from our Lord and Savior's jar
An evangelist traveling far over the countryside
With Jesus comfortably tucked in at your side
Taking the message from God's Holy Word and doing it well
Desperately trying to keep the unsaved from the fires of hell
With your wife and children traveling thousands of miles
Offering to all who hear a saving smile
For you to be at Valley Baptist Church we are really blessed
Bringing forth God's Word to see if we can pass the test
We know in heaven we'll not be near to where you will abide
My, oh my! Jesus knows you have really tried
As this started, being 6'6" tall
We are so very happy you answered God's call
Matthew 28 gives the Great Commission go and preach God's Word to all on the earth
Brother, you are sure laboring, and God will decide your worth
Preaching to us old folks as well as the young
With a goal to tell everyone to Jesus they need to belong

May God continue to keep you and your family as you travel

the nation

God will say, "Well done my true and faithful servant"

Won't that be a great sensation?

rfoltz 2/15/2004

PS May Mike, your traveling companion,

learn as much as you already known

That he too will be able to show the saving way to a lost soul

And heaven will be their only goal

The Presentor, Luis

As a presentor, we appreciate you very much
And your singing, our hearts it does touch
Yet this ministry is just the beginning
Praying there will be no ending
With the orchestra we are surely blessed
Again, we are touched, we must confess
It does not stop here; there is a Sunday school you do teach
As part of your God-given outreach
The Lord had something special for you in mind
When to Valley Baptist Church you, He did assign
Brother Luis and Sister Donna
You will never know just how much blessing you are to us
You eagerly are serving Him and so cheerful and without a fuss
Jayne and I just want you to know
What an inspiration to our hearts you have truly been
To express this we would not know where to begin
The love of our Lord and Savior does come across
And it proves you know our most
Wonderful and awesome God as boss

rfoltz 4/9/2008

The Traveling Preacher Man

Brother Rob Shealy, the preacher man
Traveling far and wide across this land
Reaching out to all he possibly can
Going from east to way out west
Challenging everyone to pass the test
He brings the message of love
Sent to all from God of heaven above
The blessed word of salvation
To this lost and dying nation
Showing with the Savior, they can have a relation
As he preaches the Word loud an clear,
May it not fall on a deaf ear
That the Lord is close by; He's very near
We'll try and remember you each day
As we go to the Lord and pray
There is a special message to relay
May this be a very happy, happy birthday

rfoltz 6/2003

A Tribute to Bob

In the few years I have known Bob,
His favorite subject was always the Bible,
The Word of God
His testimony was salvation through Jesus, God's only Son
Always hoping his witnessing was well done

He was truly sold out
As he talked with others to remove any doubt
Brought us a message each and every Sunday morn
Just in case there was one who needed to be reborn

Whether he was having coffee at Hardies, McDonald's, or on the job
He was always witnessing; yes sir, that was Bob
We will miss him each Sunday morn
However, we have no reason for alarm
We will see him again in the heavens above
Because of God's great love

He was outgoing and quite bold
He is probably with Tex, Judy, and Phil on the streets of gold
He is there doing his best in glorifying God
You can believe it because that was Bob

To his wife, Mary Sue, children, grandchildren,
and the family he left behind
It sure would please him if in heaven someday
all of those he would find

rfoltz 5/16/2007

Doctor Fauver or Brother Jeff?

Is it Doctor Fauver or Brother Jeff?
Whatever you choose, the right and not the left
We were blessed when Valley Baptist Church brought
You and your family aboard
To serve with all who assemble to worship the Lord

Your willingness and ability to head the school
To assist in the conversion of those, the Lord calls a fool
Also enabling others as witness to those you teach
Enlarging Valley's outreach

We cannot stop here
The family has brought to many lost of cheer
From the piano, organ, and a blend of voices
Enhances once more the gathering of God's choices

With Shelly, Clarissa, and Jared
Again, with these how we have fared
The singing, solo or together brings joy to the hearts
So much so, they should be number one on the charts

Being a part of Valley helps to make God's church complete

It has been proven by those who in ODACS did compete

The efforts that have been revealed

Leaves little if any doubt to be appealed

If you don't already know,

Jayne and I think you all are the best

We believe with God you have passed the test

rfoltz 4/14/2008

Mr. Zac, Our Principal, So Long

Mr. Zac, for the last 15 years you've been our great leader
Our principal, our principal in teaching us to be great readers
You've always been there for us
Your teachings we could always trust
Makes no difference if it was English, Math, or Bible
We knew if you taught it, it would be reliable
All good things must come to an end
Even though we didn't always agree,
we could still call you our friend
Wherever you go; whatever you do
We'll remember you as the head of our school
Let us take this opportunity as you leave for a better road ahead
Many of your students with your influence you've led
We want you to know around here it won't be the same
Believe us, none you have taught will ever forget your name
Even though another will be sitting in your chair
It won't be the same without you there
But remember you will always be in our prayers
Again, thanks for the guidance and direction
You did your very best
For all under your tutelage who passed through VBCS

rfoltz 6/6/2005

Two to One

Today we have gathered with family and friends to
renew our vows
To celebrate a special day here and now
But wait! We must give credit where credit is due
The Lord has shown us how to make one out of two

God has blessed us so very much
And promised to do so if we keep in touch
Jesus said, "What God has brought together let not man
put asunder"
That's very clear we need not wonder

You've proven yourself to be my perfect mate
It could have been no other way, but by fate
You will never know how happy and complete you've made my life
Since the day you said, "I do", and became my wife

Now these twenty five years have gone by with such speed
More and more every day you fill my need
Each night as we say our, "I love you's",

And seal them with a kiss
I thank the Lord for you
For giving to me a life of heavenly bliss

To you, my love, you are the one I adore
No matter how much you say you love me,
I love you much more

rfoltz 4/8/2004

Be With Them Forevermore

The Lord called; called by name
Philip, now life will never be the same
Leave behind all those aches and pains
Those things too wild for you to tame
Now you are free of the worldly care
And the things that seem unfair
Tell those who are sad not to shed a tear
Everything is perfect up here

There is a reunion about to be had
Meeting up with Helen, Galen, and others Including Mom and Dad
There are so many prayers to lift one up
So many that overrunneth the cup
We all can anxiously wait to hear our name
And life will never be the same
In that joyful reunion up there in the sky
Where we will meet again; by and by

Be comforted through Jesus' Word
One we have often heard
He will give complete peace to the heart
He will never leave us or depart
And one day a new life we will gain
Where life will never be the same
We will join the loved ones gone on before
And be with them forevermore

rfoltz 4/1/2007

Remembering Ms. Annie

One of God's chosen few
Is one of the oldest Christians I ever knew
Most devout and committed ladies to the continued service of God
Many years have passed since the Lord gave her the nod
What a testimony from one who is living The truth of her Savior, Jesus Christ
Never giving a second thought, no not once and definitely not twice
Oh, Of all the times I was terribly rude
Without the Lord in my life, my life was very crude
Bringing so much sadness into this family was so very inconsiderate
But with a forgiving heart she so graciously accepted my regrets
As only a Christian does and then forgets
May I say how happy I am that my eyes were opened and then I saw
A most unforgettable Christian lady was my mother-in-law
Thank you for your understanding and testimony of a Christian life
Who really tried to introduce me to Jesus

who finally entered my heart and

removed the strife

rfoltz 9/16/2010

May God continue to bless you today and forever after

In Appreciation to Our Pastor

What a wonderful thought
To have a pastor appreciation time
For all the preaching and lessons taught
Gives reason to honor him in this rhyme

It is an awesome job to be a pastor
Continually caring for the flock
In obedience to answer the call from the Master
To many of us it would be a shock

He is one with talents whom God leads
Counseling, visiting, and leadership
Answering wherever there are needs
Being always ready, willing, and able to make the trip

We have one such a man
Whose qualities are outstanding
Whom God has taken in hand
He fits well into God's planning

We should all be grateful for his preaching
And his concern for us

His influence is quite outreaching
And we know it is God in whom he puts his trust

Leading the congregation in praise
We are so thankful you answered God's call
A true servant He did raise
In service to us one and all

It has now been twenty-five years
Since you preached your first sermon here
You are standing firm on God's Word; doing it without any fears
And sometimes it may be with tears

May I say without any reservation
Pastor Bailey, we surely do appreciate, and we love you
For help and service you've given to many; if just in conversation
We apologize for causing you pain for wrong things we do

We extend to you from the bottom of our hearts
This congregation wants to show its love
We'll be with you 'til God calls us to depart
Then we'll congregate in God's heavenly home above

rfoltz 12/2003 rewrite from 10/2001

Why Be Baptized?

Why be Baptized? Jesus to us commanded such
Showing the Brethren with Jesus you had been in touch
Baptism will not get one to heaven, it is just a sign
That between one and the Lord things are fine.

Indicating that backward into water you did go
And coming up out of the water was not for show
Believing that Jesus died and arose just for us
For now in Him we have put our trust.

John the Baptist had Baptized Jesus before going to the cross
where He died
That being done His shed Blood for our Sins was supplied
We have now followed His command
And placed our souls into his Hand
That some Bright and Beautiful morning we'll
gather over on the Golden Strand.

rrfoltz 4/11/2011

To Those Who Wait, Ms. Annie

To get the "promised" extra strength
While not revealing the days in length.
Of your walk with Him here on earth
Only when you meet Him here on earth
Only when you meet Him face to face will you know the worth.
A beautiful time to you He has given
For the obedient way you have been livin'.
The Lord said, "On Him we are to wait"
What a blessing He has awarded
You with years numbering 98!

rfoltz 3/9/2011

The Share-A-Thon

The Share-A-Thon
By giving, we will get the job done
We are sending out a plea
Won't you please help WOTC?
No gift is too large or too small
Send it by mail or give us a call.
As we send out God's Word over the airwaves,
You will be a part of this ministry because you gave
Won't you get aboard and join in the fun?
Be a part of WOTC's Share-A-Thon!

rfoltz 10/29/2001

Now I Know Why

A funny thing happened on the way to church this morning
It suddenly came upon me with no warning.
Just how the Lord took over my life
Relieving me of all my strife.

He picked me up out of the miry clay
Showing me there was a better way.
Walking in the world of sin for many years
Everything had gone wrong, bringing many tears.

I had been such a big fool
Jesus delivered me; it was easy for Him to do
To rid me of sin in which I did abide
Things are much better now with me on His side.

While walking in the world of sin
Seemed as though evil was always inviting me in.
No longer will I bow my head and cry
The Lord Jesus answered a prayer; that's the reason why!

rfoltz 2/2002

Fishermen

Jesus called Peter and Andrew from beside the sea
Also James and John, the sons of Zebedee.
"Drop your nets and follow me,
I will make you fishers of men."
Immediately they dropped what they were doing and
followed Him.

You don't need a rod and reel
You need to know the Bible to make the appeal.
Casting God's Word into the sinners ear
Jesus to the believer will draw near
Sometimes they put up a big fight
Catching one whets one's spiritual appetite.
Follow Jesus; you won't need a rod, reel or net
For the most rewarding catch one can get.

rfoltz 10/2001

The Contract

With the Lord do you have a contract?
Confessing to Him all the unrighteousness you do lack
Asking Him to keep you on track
At anytime you may get slack.

There are no papers to sign.
He'll do it anytime
No matter what the crime
Forgiving you; that you may walk the line.

All it takes is a confession from the heart
That you have been a sinner right from the start
He is willing if you will do your part
But always remember He keeps a chart.

That chart on your life is a book
God on you; does keep a close look
Just how effective on you; His Word took
Stay firm in Him; don't get shook.

Follow Him; don't look back

Just stay in line

Do your part without any slack

Remember you don't have to sign

From your heart to the Lord; that is the contract.

Romans 10:9-10

That if thou shalt confess with thy mouth the Lord Jesus, and shalt believe in thine heart that God hath raised him from the dead, thou shalt be saved. For with the heart man believeth unto righteousness; and with the mouth confession is made unto salvation.

roltz 10/2001

What God Has Put Together

When for Adam, God made Eve
The family plan was then conceived
God's Word of the man and wife they received
It was in the garden that they believed.

Learning of the burdens they would share
Would be no more than they could bear
And to all it would be fair
Because God caused them to be there.

It was there God taught them much more
Including about the children they bore
Meting out to each their chore
To God there was an open door.

As lovers now come together
Making promises before all who gather
The devotion you make to one another
Of the storms you will have to weather.

What God has brought together; let no man put asunder
Anything that will cause them to wander
May no temptation come from yonder
No not anything, especially from down under.

May the vows be sincere
Because of the love there will be no fear
As you gaze into the other's eyes with cheer
Remember what God has put together in your heart
hold very dear

rfoltz 3/2002

Heaven's New Life

Do you often have a little spat?
Nothing too serious about this or that.
Like, "Shall we go here or there?"
Or just, "Maybe you have my chair!"

"Honey, would you do the dishes?"
"Yes, dear, anything your heart wishes.
Maybe I could sweep the floor
What else can I do? Is there something more?

Is it too hot or too cold?
Suit yourself, I can't be bold.
We get along so very good
Don't you wish everyone would?

Real life just isn't that way
But it will be one day.
When Jesus comes and takes us in
There in Heaven a new life will begin.

rfoltz 3/2002

A Prayer Group for Jesus

Each Wednesday morning at 7:30 AM
A Men's Fellowship gathers to worship Him.
The message we receive
Will strengthen us as we believe.
Going to the Lord in prayer
Knowing He is always there.
There will always be an open line
We can call on Him anytime.
BF blessed us with an open door
Here we can learn about the cross He bore.
Some consider this quite a chore
While others look to have their hearts filled with more.
So, as we eat and fellowship
Aren't you glad you made the trip?
Blessed are we for those who keep this together
Helping us one more storm to weather.
Thanks to Bob, Richard, and all the others
Who help make a challenge to the brothers.
To those we give the credit
More importantly, it is to Jesus we are indebted.

As a part of the Wednesday morning prayer group
We are in Jesus' army as throughout the world we troop.
Prayer is surely where we start
With His Word we do our part.

Matthew 7:7-8
Ask, and it shall be given you; seek, and ye shall find; knock, and it shall be opened unto you: For every one that asketh receiveth; and he that seeketh findeth; and to him that knocketh it shall be opened.

rfoltz 3/2002

His Word to the End

I was steeped in sin
Until by Jesus' mercies He took me in
And by His grace a new life I did begin.

No longer by myself do I have to fend
His laws I can no longer bend
I'll take firm stand and His Word I will always defend.

May my heart be as a den
On which I can forever depend
And will continue to the very end

rfoltz 4/2002

Out of the Darkness into Light

Out of darkness into light
Jesus freely gives us this sight
Darkness keeps in the night.

When Paul came into light from the dark,
Immediately he knew it was no lark
A new person; in ~~his~~ him there was a spark.

He said to Jesus, "What would you have me to do?"
Realizing being in the dark made him a fool
Jesus said, "Go to the city, and I'll instruct you."

Straightway his ministry began
Helping deliver those he was persecuting from sin
Fighting constantly to the very end.

When in darkness, we are blind
Until the way to Jesus we find
Where there will be no end of time.

The Narrow Way Home

This light is everywhere

You won't find any sin there

Because the same space they cannot share.

Jesus is this light you see

It is in Him we get victory

Forever then in His company we will be.

If it is our desire to do right

For our Lord and Savior it is no plight

To deliver us from this darkness into the light.

rfoltz 4/2002

A Greater Love

Years gone by brought much pleasure

Many memories we can treasure.

The most memorable to us

Is when in the Lord we put our trust.

He gave us so much with His blessings

Knowing one day we would be confessing.

Yes, there were times when we thought He let us down

Only to find out no greater love could be found.

The sinful life we did live

Wasn't much of what we had to give.

As this birthday number 71 rolls around,

Again, from god no greater love can be found.

rfoltz 3/01/2002

The Romans Road

Traveling on the Romans Road
Filled with burdens to unload
Admitting to the Lord I'm a sinner
Well seasoned, not a beginner.
I've been forgiven! What a blessing!
Walking now with Jesus; hand in hand
He knows my problems; He understands.
Now and forever I'm secure
A soul washed in His blood and made pure
Where heaven will be my eternal home.

rfoltz 12/2003

Which Mountain to Climb

Are you on Mount Ebal?
With the world standing tall.
Or is it Mount Gerizim?
All there are worshiping Him
Maybe in the valley down below
Can't make up your mind which way to go.
If on Mount Ebal, there will forever be a burning fire
Or on Mount Gerizim with the heavenly singing choir.
It will make a difference where you are
While on earth the choice is free
Which way to go; just which will it be?
Whatever the choice it will be for eternity!

Rfoltz 2/2002

Thank You Lord

Thank you Lord for the night of rest
Thank you Lord for Your very best
Thank you Lord for giving me the test.

Thank you Lord I made the grade
I'll never be alone and never afraid
A beautiful life that I'd never trade.

As the Savior, you are always near
Giving a life without fear
Thank you Lord for making it very clear.

rfoltz 12/2003

Revelation the Very End

What a wonderful occasion
To be taught the book of Revelation.
Blessed are we for the joy it brings
Because God chose to give us these things.
It was God's decision
To give to John this important vision,
That we learn of the seven stars
The seven candlesticks, just what they are
Angels and candlesticks are these
For us to know, God it does please.
Angels of the seven churches are the stars
Candlesticks, the seven churches is what they are.
There was Ephesus, Smyrna, Pergamos, Thyatira,
Sardis, Philadelphia, and Laodicea that John wrote about
Helping us relive any ill-gotten doubt.
Then the seven sealed books, seven seals, seven trumpets,
And seven vials to expose
Being of the truth, we need not suppose.
These plagues and woes describe it very clear
Remember, if saints we are, there is no fear.

Before all this, His children He will take up
That forever with Him we will sup.
Heavens opened up and on a white horse He sat Faithful and True
He was the one who offered salvation to me and you.
On the appointed "The Lord will surely return"
So for this even we need to learn
He will deliver us from the place where the fire will eternally burn.
Oh yes! To earth "The King of kings and the Lord of lords"
will come to reign.
Verifying why to earth He originally came.
It was to save a lost and dying world from the "world of sin".
Revelation reveals just how it will all end.

rfoltz 4/2003

God is the Answer

Do you have so many problems you don't know what to do?
Life looks so dim; you think you're through.
Moses had problems when at the waters of the Jordan
he got backed
He then asked the Lord to take up the slack.
With parted waters he crossed on dry ground
And on the other side, safety he found.
When those in pursuit, God opened the floodgates,
and they drowned.
Anxieties are never too big or too small
Makes no difference the Lord can cover them all.
If things seem to get you down
Don't get out of joint
The answer in God can be found.
Go to Him in prayer; He'll get the point.

rfoltz 4/2003

"The Lord is Our Shepherd"
Follow Him

The Lord is our Shepherd

We need to follow Him

When in these dark valleys and life seems so dim.

Led to the green pastures and still waters there will be peace.

His rod and staff direct to a new life, a release.

Showing all His mercy and grace so freely and willingly given

In a new home we'll be living

There will be no strife or stress

He'll give the strength to pass the test.

Remember, always the Lord is our Shepherd

when life seems so dim

All comfort and contentment comes only from Him.

rfoltz 5/2003

Take Out the Bumps

Life's road can be a very bumpy ride
With lots of hills and valleys with many ups and downs
We may swerve and run into a ditch and turn up on our side.
On the way to destruction or maybe even be Hell bound.

Wait! There may be another way for one to glide
You may have to stop and turn around
And ask Jesus to be your one and only guide.
He'll remove the aches, pains, and worries and make smiles out of what was frowns.

Get into His book; the Bible learn the law, then abide
You will know from these teachings you were lost but are found
These words from God's book to you must now be applied.
Now knowing for sure you are Heaven bound!

If you want to take the bumps out and have a smooth ride
Jesus is the only way that can be found
His Word and His alone is the only one in which you can trust and abide.
Absolutely, He's the best; no better can ever be found!

rfoltz 6/2003

Raining Again – Be Happy Rejoice

Standing, looking out the window at the ever-pouring rain
It really was coming down causing many pain.
We're so blessed, how can we ever complain?

Last winter there was so much snow
It hindered us when out we wanted to go.
But really what do we know?

Last year it was so very dry
The farmers, they wanted to cry
All our needs were met; we got by.

We pray for things to come our way
Never stopping to think what God has to say
Just let it rain and be happy and rejoice.

rfoltz 6/2003

The Beginning

Noah built an ark
With God's instructions
It was sure no lark
That it took 120 years for construction.

When it was finished
He took aboard two each of birds and animals after its kind
For the earth to replenish
Also Noah, his sons and wives, it was now their time.

God then closed the door
When the chores had been done
He caused it to rain as it had never before.
Not a more blessed family, no not one.

It rained forty days and forty nights
The Ark then floated for a year or more
While all the outside elements were closed out tight.
God was the only they are now to adore.

The rains quit and the flood subsided
To see if they were safe they sent out a dove
Still in God's Word they abided
As a witness of His love.

Coming to rest on Mount Ararat
They depart the Ark to replenish the earth
But God and Noah first had a little chat
God gave him a covenant showing His worth.

This is recorded in the book of Genesis
A great book of history
Telling all about the beginning of us
Taking away any mystery.

rfoltz 3/2002

The Light Makes Us Aware

On the road to Damascus Paul saw the light
Persecuting Christians would no longer be a delight
His eyes were opened wide
Now in God's Word he would abide.

The more we read the Bible, the more we know
The more we know, the more we find the Bible is really so.
The more we know, the more we see
The better Christians we will be.
The better Christians we are, the more we become aware
That the Lord is our Savior
Not the man upstairs.

rfoltz 2/2002

A Reason to Pray

Though we may be old and gray,
It's all the more cause to pray.
Because of His love for us
We need to turn to Him in trust.
We know He answers prayer
He's never too busy; He's always there.
Witness to all; tell them there is a need
Show them the way to heaven and plead.
Speak up; let's be bold
Rewards from His Word, we are told
Will be there with Him
"On the streets of gold".

rfoltz 2/20/2002

Nothing is Too Hard for Jesus

Jesus reached down into the miry clay
To save a lost sinner who wouldn't obey
Showing to him a life; a better way
Forgiveness, to kneel and pray.

There would now be another direction
One offering everlasting protection.
Leading to the ultimate life of perfection
All because for the sinner, His affection.

There where impurities to be worked out
Jesus could do it; there was no doubt
For within Him there is plenty of clout
We then have reason to rejoice with a shout.

A new saint has now been born
Out of life that was so forlorn
In the body a Christian will adorn
With radiant beauty all neat and shorn.

We may say it's impossible for God to do
To change a sinner like us; what would He have when through?
There is really no reason to be blue
After all, He made me and you.

Matthew 19:26
But Jesus beheld them, and said unto them, With men this is impossible; but with God all things are possible.

rfoltz 11/2003

Do As God Directs; Not As I Do

Each Sunday morning we come and fill a pew
That's what all good Christians do
Sit and listen so very attentive
As the preacher gives instructions on how to live.

Now he didn't just make this up
God has blessed him with a full cup
Directing him to preach the real stuff
And we will never have enough.

The preacher searches the Scriptures through and through
To bring to us a message that is true.
God has laid this on his heart
His Word which he does impart.

Are we set in our ways
As was Pharaoh in the olden days?
Is the heart hardened; do we resist this teaching?
Which the man of God has been preaching.

The Narrow Way Home

We listen and store it away in the brain
And never bringing it up again.
Let's be obedient and do what we are to do
As he preaches to us while sitting in the comfortable pew.

Are we callus or do we not hear well,
Or are we just waiting the closing bell?
Don't go down in defeat
Be sincere because in heaven there is a better seat.

God is always the same yesterday, tomorrow, even so today
Now on your knees don't forget as you pray.
Always asking for wisdom to direct your way
And follow orders as He directs; no mind what others may say.

In Revelation we are told
"That we would be hot or cold"
We need to be outgoing and bold
To save the lost and dying soul.

rfoltz 8/2003

Floating On Cloud Nine

It all happen so very fast
When the Lord I did ask
To forgive me of the sins past
Always and Forever, ever to Last.

I didn't have to stand in line
Quickly He said, you are fine
Those terrible things are now all behind
That is why I'm floating on cloud nine.

His word does last forever and will never roam
Our minds can be fertile loam
When sharing with others that HEAVEN is now our HOME.

As Jesus our Savior; us He did find
What a wonderful reason to be
"FLOATING ON CLOUD NINE".

r foltz 6/15/2011

Stepping on Toes

Last Sunday when I awoke
I said, "I'm going to church today; that's no joke".
Yes! That is what I'm going to do
I'll go to Valley Baptist Sunday school.
I had breakfast and got into my Sunday clothes
With steel-toed shoes to protect my toes.

All dressed up, off I went
This time of fellowship, would it be well spent?
The teacher taught about Jesus and His chosen twelve
How everywhere they'd go on God's Word they would dwell.
Leading to salvation is what he chose
That was when he really came down hard on my toes.

It turned out to be a most interesting class
But it all went so very fast.
He asked us to stay for the preaching hour
To enjoy the preaching and the singing of the choir.
I decided, "Why not?" It may do me good
Just maybe I'd learn more of what I should.

The Narrow Way Home

Maybe the preacher's sermon would be one of those
That wouldn't be too hard on my toes.

The choir and congregation did beautifully sing
At a Baptist church they will never forget the offering.
After the second song, the choir came down
Greeting all who were near around.
Now that is the way an opening goes
That wasn't too hard on my toes.

Then came the preacher's turn
Giving a sermon that could cause some to squirm.
He told us sinners we all are
I never thought it would really take an hour.
Boy! Did I hope he would soon close
Because he was all over my toes!

The preacher got carried away on salvation,
And I thought he'd never quit.
Even though the pews were comfortable, and I could hear
Good from where I sit.

For any who needed salvation or to repent he gave an altar call
Making it available to one and all.

Now that is just how it goes
As he walks about on your toes.

That Sunday teacher and the preacher really made me wonder
A point that I would take time to ponder.
I decided to go back again Sunday night
I wasn't convinced I had it all right.
As these morning services came to a close,
The preacher again had walked all over my toes.

I came back for the evening service
Being uncomfortable and a bit nervous.
Everyone seemed cordial and welcomed me back
Relieved the pressure and it took up some slack.
There was just no time to dose
Because they were always on your toes.

Convicted of the sinner that I am, I could no longer sit still
God worked on my heart to follow His will.
Finally on Wednesday night I accepted Jesus as Lord and Savior!
Look at me now, you can see the changes in my behavior.
Valley Baptist I'm glad I chose
They sure are not afraid to step on anyone's toes.

In this limerick we could include the evangelist that's for sure
As he travels all over from shore to shore,
Or wherever he goes
He takes God's messages and continues stepping on toes!

rfoltz 1/5/2004

Why I Don't Sing in the Choir or A Man From Songtucket

There was once a man from Songtucket
Who couldn't carry a tune in a bucket
He was so saddened that he sat down and cried and cried
He had done his best; he tried and tried
He wanted to reveal his happiness by singing with joy
But he never could sing, not even as a boy

While in the choir, and they would sing a hymn
Someone would sing quite loud to sing over him
Forlorn and dejected on his way home
He got a notion; he delightfully would say it by the way of a poem
He read and wrote poems each and every day
Expressing his joy in a most entertaining way
So now he needs no longer to carry a bucket
He became a poet, this man from Songtucket

rfoltz 11/2002 rewrite 9/18/2010

Sprinkled, Dunked & BAPTIZED!
"Into the True Light"

"This day in Baptist History II", by David L. Cummins has many references to Adoniram and Ann Judson, mostly concerning the Missions to Burma in 1807. August 27th gives an account of Adoniram closely examining the scriptures as Ann joined in. It took nearly four months for them to become convinced that "Immersion of a professing believer is the only Christian Baptism".

Becoming aware of the controversy and disagreement among Christians, including Baptist, sprinkling, being dunked and Baptized the proper and accepted way of the Fundamental Baptist, I had been sprinkled, and dunked, but never by the Fundamental Baptist way.

As a child I was sent to Sunday school and on the occasional preaching in either the A.M. service or maybe the alternating afternoon preaching time as it would be scheduled according to the other Churches in sharing of the Preacher. It never became a reality or much less, a care or I saw a need aside from the importance until

I was quite a bit older. I was completely Bible Illiterate, never read a Bible until I got into a Bible study.

This was in the "Reform Church", (now the UCC), with a requirement that one must be 13 years old to become a member of the church. I do not remember if Baptism (sprinkled) was required or not, however I had been sprinkled. Age made no difference, rather a day old or older, one was sprinkled with a few drops of water over the head.

I know I had a desire to be part of that church even though I did not understand why. I do know that the fear of the Lord was instilled in me; yes, I was scared of GOD. It was during this time that I left the church for many years. I was 21 years old before God made another appearance in my life, and that would be only temporary then.

After leaving the Reformed Church as a teenager and joining the Army, only then would I attend any church other than when I was shipping out to go overseas or to a combat zone. Then I went a time or two. There would be none of which I would become involved. This is what I call "Fox hole Religion", fear of what lay ahead, fear of the unknown and need of personal assurance with God though not a believer.

After a while, in the new assigned area I got into the routine and became familiar in my surroundings. I knew the area and soon I was back to the same old way as before. The "old man" soon became my way of life again. The "Old Me" was still there and had reared its ugly head again.

When I was married the first time, another religion came into my life, "The Brethren Church". I became quite active in it until I got disillusioned and could not handle a man of God being dishonest with the church. I knew enough that one must obey God and should not be dishonest. However, in the mean time I had to be baptized again. I was baptized (dunked, going down forward) by the Rev. Pastor Brother Ed Miller. Brother Ed was a great preacher of God for whom I had great respect. It was not him that I became disillusioned with. He followed the Brethren Church as close as he could in their dispensation. Still I did not know the way of salvation. <u>I needed to know the way to make the right commitment.</u>

This would be a good time to relate an occurrence in my life while in the local Hospital as a patient. A Baptist Preacher visited me and as he was about to leave he had prayer. He did not ask if he could, he just prayed. It was then and there I said, "They will never make a Baptist out of me". He was too pushy, was I every more than fooled! The Lord sure has His way when we are disobedient to Him. I was Bible illiterate. Still I never read a Bible until I got into a Bible study.

After the second marriage, we realized there was something amiss in our lives. We needed to get back into church. She had been a dedicated Lutheran an also sprinkled. It was then that we joined the church that I had grown up in, A Reform Church, now the UCC. There, we soon realized that we were not being taught what the Bible had to say. It was our desire to know the truth and we were not getting it.

God knows our needs and sent us a teacher who came into our home and taught us. She was well qualified, she had a B.A. from "Bob Jones University" and a M.A. from Moody Bible Institute, and she fed us the proper teachings. We continued for four and half years with a Bible study in our home each Wednesday night.

It was about this time we realized that we had never accepted the Lord as Savior. Trying to get all the learning to keep us in line, we watched TV Preachers. One day in June of 1981 in front of the TV, we got on our knees, admitted to Jesus we were sinners, and repented of our past sins and to please forgive us. <u>He did! We are His children</u>.

Not only was she very good and sound teacher but also had many people praying for our salvation, which would lead us to a Bible Believing and Preaching Church. Those prayers were about to be answered. We were invited to join the Valley Baptist Church. A couple visited us from Valley Baptist church, Mr. & Mrs. Ivor Crisman who invited us to join them in worship. We did! We liked what we heard and came back again and again. We were very hungry to learn and to satisfy a needed spiritual appetite. <u>God leads His poor children along.</u>

After of attending (about a year), we met with the preacher who informed us we would need to be BAPTIZED as our other so-called baptism would not be accepted in Valley Baptist Church. We accepted that, agreed, and were baptized. We answered an ALTER CALL to join and then became members of Valley Baptist

Church in 1982. We are now being continually fed from God's word three times a week, by an outstanding "Man of God", Jim Bailey, now for over 30 years.

I had been sprinkled, dunked (forward), but never in the proper manner as the only way is backward, down and up in accordance to the way John BAPTIZED JESUS. If we will read about Jesus, we will find He was buried and rose up to be with the Father. Coming up out of the water, Matt: 3: 17 and lo, a voice from heaven, saying, "This is My beloved son, in whom I am well pleased".

It is our desire to follow Him as closely as we can. In Matthew 19: 16-24 Jesus told the Young Rich Ruler who asked Jesus "what good thing shall I do that I may have eternal life", "Jesus told him to sell all he had and follow Him". This pointed out that we make HIM first in our lives. He is to come before anything we may want or have and worship Him. Yes, this includes our house, car, boat, money, anything that would come between our God and us including our FAMILY.

Not being baptized will not keep one out of heaven; however, it is a command of our Lord, Jesus Christ to follow Him. Baptism is a sign to all that we are SAVED, A CHILD OF GOD, and will forever be in His care. Hebrew 13: 5b says, "He will never leave thee nor forsake thee". **It must be sincere, from the heart.** II Cor. 5:17 "Therefore, if any man is in Christ, he is a new creature; old things are passed away; behold all things become new".

John 1:4 & 5 "In Him was life, the life was the light of darkness. And the light shines in darkness, and the darkness did not comprehend it". Receiving the light makes all the difference in the world, you can see where you are going. Jesus is the Spiritual light that opens our understanding of the scriptures. It was not until I received this light and truly understood the need for salvation. Saul in Acts 9: 3 & 4 had been blinded by a ~~that~~ light came upon him and he then started to serve the Lord. In vv six Saul said, "Lord what wilt thou have me to do". Read the book of John. It has much to say about the Light. There is no substitute on earth for this **LIGHT** as some do say, Jesus is the **TRUE LIGHT**. <u>The Bible makes this very clear.</u>

Walk hand and hand with Him and He will carry you through. (There may be times when there will only be one set of footprints, that was when He was carrying you). I had been Sprinkled, then Dunked, and finally I saw the Light and came out of the darkness.. We were then immersed and rose up in Prayer and I wait now to hear "God say, well done my faithful servant". I will Serve Him and know as He has promised, "He will never leave me nor forsake me"

It was in 1981 that I started reading the Bible through at least once a year. I started growing and continue nearly 31 years later. My inspiration keeps getting deeper and deeper in His word by learning more and more...

As I have previously mentioned "I saw the Light". Saul in Acts 9 was blinded by the LIGHT of JESUS CHRIST. Jesus said, "Saul, Saul why persecutes thou me"? Saul said, who art thou Lord"? And the

Lord said I am Jesus whom thou persecute; it is hard for thee to kick against the pricks. VV6 and he trembling and astonished said, Lord, what will wilt thou have me to do? And the Lord said unto him, arise, and go into the city, and it shall be told what thee what thou must do. This I repeat because it is very important that follow Jesus direction.

See the Journey of a Lost Man Traveling The Broad Road

Randolph Foltz
Feb. 28 2011

A Solemn Plea

With coupled hands firmly planted on the Bible
And a sorrowful heart, we ask for revival.
From our bended knees
Bring forth our sinful pleas
To be forgiven!
Of the sin-filled lives that we have been livin'
Emptying our souls filled with leaven
Upon Your calling we can join you in Heaven!
To You, Oh Lord, is Our Plea!
That is from Jayne and Me.
4/25/2012

CPSIA information can be obtained at www.ICGtesting.com
Printed in the USA
BVOW11s1054220814

363772BV00007B/20/P